The Nature of
Science

The Nature of Science

SECOND EDITION

Frederick Aicken

HEINEMANN
Portsmouth, New Hampshire

Heinemann

A division of Reed Elsevier, Inc.
361 Hanover Street, Portsmouth, NH 03801-3912

Offices and agents throughout the world

Library of Congress Cataloging-in-Publication Data

Aicken, Frederick.
    The nature of science/Frederick Aicken. — 2nd ed.
       p. cm.
    Includes bibliographical references.
       ISBN 0-435-08310-4
        1. Science — Philosophy.   2. Science — History.   I. Title.
Q175.A336 1991
501 — dc20   90 — 46236
                                                 CIP

Designed by Jenny Jensen Greenleaf
Printed in the United States of America
00 99 98 97 2 3 4 5

for Catherine and Daniel again—
and now also for
Anna, Alexander, and Esther

Contents

Preface to the Second Edition

I continue to feel that we need, in both formal and informal education, an approach to science that will show its human face and therefore its importance to each one of us. I like to think that this book, in its first edition, both underlined that need and went some way to satisfying it.

It is gratifying to be able to apply second thoughts to a project, particularly after the opportunity to consider criticisms of the first. I hope that this new edition will give clearer guidance and more direct stimulation to those students, teachers in training, and established teachers who read it. I must remind them that the book is not a history of scientific ideas; it is intended to be a commentary on such ideas and on related issues, all of which can be fully explored elsewhere. Neither is my coverage of these ideas comprehensive; I hope that the existence of gaps will spur readers to fill them.

Once again I thank Graham Taylor who read the first draft of the book and made suggestions for its improvement. I must also thank Toby Gordon who invited me to prepare the present edition; her enthusiasm in collecting critical opinions from American readers was most persuasive and welcome. Whatever faults the book may still have, it is all the better for the help of these editors.

CHAPTER ONE

Introduction

Ninety-nine percent of man's story is the story of his science.
— *John Ferguson*

Man is what he has done.
— *Berthold Brecht*

Science is the attempt to make the chaotic diversity of our sense experience correspond to a logically uniform system of thought.
— *Albert Einstein*

We should ask ourselves why the views of Copernicus, the discoveries of Galileo, the understanding and syntheses of Newton, should so greatly have resonated through European society, so greatly have altered the words with which men spoke of themselves and their destiny.
— *Robert Oppenheimer*

I do not know what I may appear to the world, but to myself I seem to have been only like a boy playing on the sea-shore, and diverting myself in now and then finding a smoother pebble or a prettier shell than ordinary, whilst the great ocean of truth lay all undiscovered before me.
— *Isaac Newton*

The quick harvest of applied science is the usable process, the medicine, the machine. The shy fruit of pure science is Understanding.
— *Lincoln Barnett*

It is a mistake to believe that a science consists in nothing but conclusively proved propositions, and it is unjust to demand that it should. That is a demand only made by those who feel a craving for authority in some form and a need to replace the religious catechism by something else, even if it be a scientific one.
— *Sigmund Freud*

We have a long-standing and highly successful tradition of inquiry devoted to the development of knowledge and technology ... We have so far failed even to develop traditions of inquiry devoted to helping us solve our problems of living in co-operative, just and humane ways.
— *Nicholas Maxwell*

You teach your daughters the diameters of the planets, and wonder when you have done that they do not delight in your company.
— *Dr. Johnson*

Lives of scientists oft remind us
We can make our own sublime —
If they don't blow up Creation
Leaving naught but Space and Time.
— *Bob Stannard*

Questions . . .

What is truth?

What is science?

'Ninety-nine percent of man's story is the story of his science.' Do you agree?

We create tools. To what extent have tools created us?

We are told that God created human kind. Is it not more likely that humans created God?

Should science be an integral part of general education?

Science in history

Some years ago I came across the text of a lecture given by a professor of classics to a conference of science teachers in Ghana. The subject was Science and History and an early sentence leapt out of the page and stuck in my mind: 'Ninety-nine percent of man's story is the story of his science.' This was startling even to me who could not accept the separation of the arts from the sciences in our daily lives and, in particular, our education. But before I had reached the end of the first paragraph I was firmly convinced of the truth of the statement.

Early influence of science on society

Human beings have been on this planet for little over half a million years of which recorded history has documented only the last six thousand. During all of this time, we can trace their progress largely through their control of the environment, that is, by applied science. We see this first in the succession of ways in which humans obtained food. Initially, they merely found and gathered it; then they hunted it; later still, they grew it. They were learning to interfere with the rest of the natural world and to change it for their own benefit. They would cease to rely on their own unaided strength and would begin to dominate and use animals, many of them larger and stronger. They would no longer have to find edible plants for survival but would sow seeds in areas of their choice. Humans would cease to be nomads and become settlers.

Even at this early stage science had begun to affect the structure of society. The earliest societies depended on finding and gathering food and were ruled by women; although there was no difference between the sexes in their ability to obtain food, women were obviously of supreme importance in producing new members of the society. But when hunting replaced food gathering, women lost their earlier status because of their weaker physiques and frequent pregnancies. Later, in settled communities which practised agriculture, they regained it; legends associated with the discovery and cultivation of corn refer to goddesses rather than gods.

Development of primitive scientific method

By trial-and-error, even before the formation of the first settlements, humans had invented crude weapons and tools and embarked on a primitive technology. Upon becoming settlers, we learned to control fire, to become cooks, and eventually chemists. Humans discovered copper and its alloy bronze and, in the areas of the Middle East where copper ores were available, the ancient civilizations of Egypt and Mesopotamia were built. Before that, we had noticed that tree trunks could be made to roll and were able to invent the wheel and later the pulley. In coping with the problems arising from these devices, we began to be physicists. The use of wheels made the craft of pottery easier and the increased output of pots made us into entrepreneurs. Wheeled transport allowed us to explore more widely; we discovered new substances like iron ores which were more plentiful and more widespread than those of copper and we gradually learned to extract from them the first crude iron and steel. But however crude, they were used to topple the Egyptian civilizations because their abundance challenged the dependence of those civilizations on the more rare copper.

When we watch scientists at work — even those primitive scientists with their crude wheels and rough metals — we forget

that much of their activity is mental. Problems arising from the use
of early tools developed the human brain and this increased the
ability to think and made easier the solving of new problems. This
was the construction of an early form of what we now call scientific
method. In the new communities which grew their own food and
raised their own animals, there was more time to do nothing, to
make plans for future activity, or to wonder about changes in the
weather, the night skies, or the seasons. The majority of people
would not have worried about reasons for these changes; they
would be interested only in, say, choosing the best time to sow
seeds. But some must have sought understanding.

Women, nursing their babies, might begin to look inward as
well as outward; they would notice similarities between the phases
of the moon and their own biological rhythms. They might also
speculate on the contrast between their feelings of maternal
tenderness and the warlike emotions of some of the men. Almost
certainly there would be an element of fear in all these musings
because humans, apparently superior to other forms of life, were
still very much at the mercy of storms, floods, and famine. If only
to get rid of such fear, we began to look for explanations. We had
begun the search for truth which, thousands of years later, still
absorbs us.

The first theories

The observed changes gradually revealed more or less fixed patterns.
The dark of the night sky was always banished by the rising of the
sun, although the sun was seen to be higher in the sky as the days
grew longer and warmer. After the chill of winter, plants seemed
to rise from the dead but as the sun once again began to sink lower
in the midday sky, they would once more show signs of approaching
death. In the ensuing periods of winter's darkness, early humans
must often have wondered if they, too, were doomed. Their time
on earth was very short and their growing awareness of seasonal
changes was limited by the sparse information passed on by their
elders. They began dimly to realize that there were forces of nature
that might never be controlled. Primitive weapons were useless
and all people could do was invent stories—to try to understand,
possibly to avoid, the effects of these forces. They assumed that,
high up in the sky, there must be supernatural beings who withdrew
heat and light or hurled thunderbolts as punishment. Perhaps
these beings could be placated by offering gifts—a lamb, a cow,
even a child. As the days continued to shorten their fears grew;
they devised magic rituals, built bonfires, tried to imitate the
imagined processes of destruction and also some actions which

might overcome them. And their efforts seemed to work. In the depths of wintry gloom, at a time when some of us now celebrate Christmas, it was just possible to see that the days had begun to lengthen, that light and life seemed to have been reborn. Later, about the time which we now call Easter, it was obvious that some form of resurrection had taken place, that life had somehow emerged from a dead world. Could all this have been the result of prayers and rituals?

Early science and the supernatural

We can see here the beginnings of a split view of natural mysteries. On the one hand, the mundane problems of everyday life had formed a rudimentary problem-solving, thought-provoking system which, in a more refined form, we would call scientific method. On the other hand, deeper mysteries had inspired a fabric of fictional tales which evolved into mythology, the beginnings of literature, drama, and religions. Moreover, the increase of intelligence and of imagination resulting from the scientific experience was now applied to the fiction and made it increasingly complex. Witch doctors became the wise men of their communities and they dealt with all problems, scientific and emotional. Later, churches became the centres of all forms of scholarship, even that part, the scientific, which we now study separately. The result was that all natural mysteries and possible interpretations became entangled with the supernatural. The less complicated—for example, the sequences of night and day and of the seasons—were gradually explained by the movement of the sun relative to the earth and, whatever the origin of the moving force, the movement itself was simple enough for rational explanation. Other mysteries were less easily explained. The way human begins behave, the complexity and power of their emotions, were not so predictable or understandable. Nevertheless it was assumed that human beings, like the seasons, were influenced by the sun and other heavenly bodies; but, whereas the science of astronomy gradually and accurately deepened our view of the universe, astrology (which sought to explain human behaviour in terms of planetary movement) was to remain shrouded in ambiguity and vagueness.

Has modern science made too much progress?

The success of astronomy accelerated the progress of science in many directions, and science slowly displaced religion as a focus for the explanation of natural mysteries. The scientific revolution of the fifteenth and sixteenth centuries was followed, in the Western world, by an industrial (or technological) revolution which was both a manifestation of scientific progress and an encouragement for new scientific endeavour. The majority of people who, generations earlier, would have had to scrape a living, now enjoyed material comfort and relative wealth. It seemed to many of the intellectual minority that a new age, a golden era of unlimited scientific progress, had begun.

But others were doubtful. To them, the pendulum had merely swung from one extreme to another, from a wholly religious view of the universe to a wholly mechanical and materialistic. Neither position was satisfactory. In the late twentieth century most of us would probably agree. Our interference with nature seems to have gone too far; even if we are no longer threatened by immediate nuclear annihilation, we are in danger of slowly killing our planet by pollution from both poisonous industrial waste and the relatively innocuous carbon dioxide which we—and our cars—pump into the atmosphere at an alarming rate. We continue to enjoy the benefits of science yet we have become disenchanted with it, just as our ancestors slowly turned away from the more simplistic messages of religion.

The progress of science is reflected in our maturing

Faced with scientific gloom we may close our eyes to cosmic or planetary problems and try to get on with our daily lives as well as we can. But we may find little comfort in so doing because the historical swings between irrational beliefs and blind trust in science are mirrored in individual experience. Children first learn to control their bodily movements by trial-and-error. They gradually become aware of patterns in the constant change around them. In trying to cope with these they begin to think for themselves and many seem to cultivate an inner world of fantasy which makes sense of the world outside. They are frequently beset by fears which the experience of their parents cannot dispel; they try to deal with these by their own means, perhaps by devising explanations involving imaginary beings and fantastic events. In fact, they are creating their own myths or, some would say, re-creating myths which have comforted uncounted generations of ancestors.

Gradually they begin to think more rationally and they may fall under the spell of science. They marvel at the accuracy with which science has put mortals and materials into space and they are enthusiastic about the possibilities of travel to the edges of the universe and through time itself. They are dazzled and beguiled by the wealth of gadgetry—from personal stereos to the most sophisticated computers—which science has indirectly provided. They will become aware of the horrors which the misuse of science has led to, but they cling to the belief that these can be reversed, that science can still feed the hungry, cure the sick, and save the planet. Yet most do become disillusioned. They begin to look on the scientist as a latter-day witch-doctor, a clever manipulator of mysterious equipment and even of human beings. They treat the scientist with respect, even with awe, but with more than a little suspicion. The scientist is needed but not liked, and has become both super-human and less than human.

Distrust of modern science

In particular, children distrust scientists because of the doubts they offer in place of the certainties children seek. Scientists have poured scorn on religious belief but that, at least, had offered comfort whereas science austerely claims that there are no certainties, no absolute truths. So the adolescents of today, increasingly aware of inner fears as they struggle toward maturity, look in vain for the answers at the back of the scientific book. How, then, do they know that they are on the right track? How can they be sure of their way through life if they have no reliable guide?

Small wonder, then, that so many of today's young people shun science. If they are students, they may prefer the emotional and creative satisfactions of music, poetry, or literature. Or they may look on their studies as the surest path to the best possible job or career and postpone any concern for 'job satisfaction.' They may find that they spend more and more time looking for some form of escape from an increasingly boring routine. Some will find it in alcohol and other drugs; a few will discover refuge in religions, perhaps even in those 'phoney' religions fringing on the occult. They will all have found at least a temporary reward in warmth, excitement, even humanity which they do not find in the cold materialism of science. They will admit that science is not in itself malignant. Like its own products—fire, steel, nuclear energy, the laser beam—it can be used for human benefit as well as for destruction. But, these young people seem to say, let those who are interested in it get on with it; it's not for us.

Why we must all understand science

But it *is*. We have all been shaped by science and science pervades so much of our experience that we must try to understand it if only to have some share in controlling its use. How many of us know, for example, the complex background to the 'greenhouse effect' of that carbon dioxide emission? Do we really understand the dangers and the possible advantages of nuclear power? And what are the consequences of doing without it? Are we all clear in our minds about the threat of too much cholesterol in our diets? About the benefits and drawbacks of irradiated food? About the dangers of sugar, smoking, sex? We cannot opt out of such problems by leaving the solutions to fate or to someone else. It is our duty to ourselves, as well as our duty as citizens, to ensure that these problems are properly addressed by politicians, business people, or scientists themselves.

And even if we do opt out, we cannot escape the need to make our own private decisions each day of our lives. We are already aware that nothing in life is certain and that we take risks at practically every moment. We may decide to leave everything to chance with an envious thought for those who still believe in immunity from danger through religious faith. It may not have occurred to us that science, having revealed so much uncertainty, has faced the consequences. Could it therefore teach us how to assess risks — of being involved in accidents, of being infected by diseases? Could it suggest evasive action? Then, it would be up to each one of us to decide what action to take.

The need for balance between science and the arts

Clearly we cannot all call ourselves scientists, but we certainly cannot claim to be non-scientists. If we could transport ourselves back in time to the fourteenth century we would be less surprised by the physical appearance of our new horizons than by the strange ways in which our new neighbours would behave or think. Modern science has transformed not merely the surface of the Western world but the very personalities of its inhabitants.

We may instinctively resent the allegation that ninety-nine percent of our thinking is scientific until we begin to analyze our thought processes. When we are ill or injured, do we seek cures through medicine or mysticism? When we think about the wonders of nature, do we not take for granted large parts (at least) of scientific explanations of the origins of the universe and of life on planet Earth? When we feel angry at the misuse of Earth's resources, do we recommend prayer or a more responsible use of science as a remedy? And when we approach everyday problems (imagining first a possible explanation, then testing it and subsequently confirming or rejecting it), aren't we making an approximation to scientific method?

We must remember that the relative importance of this scientific side to our behaviour cannot be assessed by mere arithmetic. In the baking of bread the quantity of yeast is negligible yet we all know the effect on the bread if the yeast is accidentally left out. Can it be that, in our individual lives and educational systems, we have too frequently left the human element out of our study of science and failed to consider more rationally and less emotionally our view of religion and the arts? Could this account for science and art existing as two cultures, for a lack of wholeness in our own personalities?

Science in schools

Most people's ideas about science stem from experience in schools. Science has taken up more and more of the timetable in recent years (politicians tell us that 'the country needs more scientists') and all children, by the age of eleven at most, have begun mysterious rituals with Bunsen burners and test-tubes. Yet the majority will not become scientists and, while they regard the scientific few with a mixture of envy and admiration, they often resent any further pressure to include more science in their studies. All those experiments with silver paper on leaves of plants, all those bangs and smells in chemistry labs, all that rubbing of plastic rods with cat fur—no wonder most of us end up with the vague belief that science is a modern form of witchcraft.

In his essay 's' Times What? the English humorist Paul Jennings describes his schoolboy attitude to those science specialists who 'had the right, detached attitude to matter which is basically white or yellow powder in menacing little bottles. They weren't afraid of breaking it down, whereas I felt, even then, doubtless in a deplorably primitive and superstitious way, that it was best left alone .... And look how frightening it gets when you break down the sodium and chlorine into all those protons, mesons, crotons, cretins, morons, anti-morons, etc. Those boys with fountain pens that never made blots, those boys whose socks never came down, they could make matter sit up and beg for them' (Golden Oddlies, A Methuen Humour Classic, o.p.).

That was written forty years ago and the memories recorded occurred about twenty years earlier. But they still have a familiar ring. Because of the very structure of school science, students get a cramped and distorted view of what the subject really is about. Science is not a mass of information to be memorized for examinations and, with a little luck, partially understood by a few. It is an evolving process of thought which has revealed this information and which continues to expose fresh mysteries, large and small. The study of science should, therefore, give each of us the same intellectual pleasure as the unravelling of a puzzle — a sense of achievement which is usually missing from school science because of the awareness that the solutions already exist.

Furthermore, school science is not overtly related to other subjects. The study of history often proceeds without mention of the scientific background of particular ages — yet it is science that has altered people's views about their position in the world and in the universe. Similarly, literature reflects these views and their implications in human behaviour and thought; it would be impossible to make a full study of the works of Shakespeare, for example, without knowing something about the upheaval in scientific thought which took place in his lifetime. And when we consider religious education we find a deep gulf between the two subjects. In science it is essential that the seeker of truth must be open-minded about the outcome of his enquiries; but in religious studies the solution, too often, has already been decided and the function of study is to confirm it.

What this book sets out to do

Despite many honourable attempts to remove it, there is still a split in our educational system between the arts and the sciences which corresponds to a division in our minds between the intellect and the emotions. This is obviously unhealthy both for society as a whole and for the individuals within it. An unbalanced study of science tends to produce the type of person who enthusiastically collects components for a perfect hi-fi assembly but who, when it is built, shows no interest in the range of sublime music which is available. The fact that many graduates in science are exceptions to this statement is a tribute to the nagging persistence of the human spirit and not always to formal education.

In this book we shall not only ask 'What *is* science?' but 'What is science *for*?' I have been pleased by the response of some readers of the first edition who, having been taught separate sciences at school, had hitherto no clear idea about the nature of science as a whole. There were also those who, having hated the very word 'science' at school, now wished that they could have followed a course of the history of scientific ideas to complement their interest in the arts.

But this book is not a text-book on the history of science or on scientific method. It is a series of linked essays on these and similar themes. One or two scientific topics are treated in some detail for the purpose of illustration but the idea is to provide a personal commentary on topics that the reader may have already met or may be stimulated to explore elsewhere. The contents of the essays necessarily overlap but each is reasonably complete in itself. Each is preceded by quotations and questions to provoke interest, thought, and discussion which the essay itself attempts to widen and deepen. There is also a (deliberately) sketchy chronological table to provide an historical perspective. Most important of all there are suggestions for further reading which will help to rectify the book's omissions, simplifications, and superficialities. These would be inexcusable in a work of deeper scholarship but are, I hope, justifiable in a book which aims not to satisfy but to stimulate.

CHAPTER TWO

Facts

JACK: That, my dear Algy, is the whole truth, pure and simple.
ALGERNON: The truth is rarely pure and never simple.
— *Oscar Wilde*

Science is built up with facts, as a house with stones. But a collection of facts is no more a science than a heap of stones is a house.
— *J. H. Poincaré*

Facts, apart from their relationships, are like labels on empty bottles.
— *Sven Halla*

Knowledge comes from noticing resemblances and recurrences in the events that happen around us.
— *Wilfred Trotter*

It is an old maxim of mine that when you have excluded the impossible, whatever remains, however improbable, must be the truth.
— *'Sherlock Holmes' through Conan Doyle*

Seek simplicity and distrust it.
— *A. N. Whitehead*

Error is all around us and creeps in at the least opportunity. Every method is imperfect.
— *C. J. H. Nicolle*

Certainty is an illusion. You have to get used to the idea that things are probable or improbable. If only we could attain a feeling of happiness when we recognize that we live in a probabilistic world, we'd be so much better off.
— *Allen Walker Read*

Lest men suspect your tale untrue,
Keep probability in view.
— *John Gay*

In an ideal biological experiment where all variables but the experimental variables are controlled perfectly, and the experimental variables are measured accurately, the organism does what it likes.

Addendum 1. Sometimes.
— *Finagle's Laws*

When it comes to atoms, language can be used only as in poetry. The poet, too, is not nearly so concerned with describing facts as with creating images.
— *Niels Bohr*

Questions . . .

What is a fact?

Why do we need so many provisos, exceptions, qualifications in trying to state the facts exactly? Why do we need 'the small print'?

How reliable are scientific facts?

What is experimental error? What does an engineer mean by 'tolerance' in reference to his measurements?

Why, in *The Merchant of Venice*, was Shylock unable to demand his pound of flesh?

What is 'the uncertainty principle'?

How do scientists arrive at 'the facts'?

What is a scientific law? How does it resemble, or differ from, a law that we must obey in our everyday lives?

In what ways is a research scientist like a detective?

What evidence would you accept as certain in a murder trial? That of eye-witnesses? Of cameras or tape-recorders? Confession from the accused?

How reliable are 'the facts' we get from newspapers or newsreels?

The scientist works like a detective

'Let's begin with the facts' is an admirable start to any discussion or investigation. Unfortunately it may not always be as easy as it looks. A scientist in search of truth may be usefully compared with a detective unravelling the mysteries of a crime — but often a crime which has been committed some time ago in circumstances which have since changed. That famous fictional detective Sherlock Holmes said: 'The difficulty is to detach the framework of fact — of absolute, undeniable fact — from the embellishments of theorists and reporters. We are suffering from a plethora of surmise, conjecture, and hypothesis.'

Consider the following cases: A man lies dead, a woman stands over him with a knife in her hand; is she guilty of his murder? Not if the man died of a heart attack when threatened; not if he is subsequently found to have been poisoned by someone else. A boy fires a pistol at a teacher; the teacher is shot dead. But the boy's pistol is found to have been loaded with blanks and the bullet which killed the teacher was fired from someone else's gun.

Unreliability of eye-witnesses

Such incidents may be the stuff of thrillers but they serve to remind us of the dangers of jumping too quickly to conclusions, of not looking for as many facts as possible, of seeing only what we want to see. All of us are blessed with imagination, by which we are able to link facts or observations into patterns; but it is easy to form a pattern prematurely and so exclude information which might lead to a different pattern. The second incident recalls uncomfortable memories of the assassination of President Kennedy in Dallas in 1963; the testimony of hundreds of eyewitnesses, all eager to tell the truth, the whole truth, and nothing but the truth, pointed to the guilt of one man. But evidence from tape-recorders and cameras created doubts and the truth about the killing is still far from clear despite a multiplicity of facts, some of them contradictory.

Can the camera lie?

Even the evidence of recording machines is not absolutely reliable. In spite of claims that are often made, the camera *can* lie when it is used for deliberate photographic tricks. Normally, it records what it 'sees' but, by collaboration with our imaginations, it persuades us to *interpret* the resultant picture; once again, we see what we are made to see. When we watch a newsreel we see only what the photographer happens to, chooses to, or is told to photograph. What does not appear on the screen may be just as important as what is actually presented. And any newsreel, however long, has been cut and possibly rearranged to fit the scheme of the producer; the selection of images and their order of appearance suggest to our imaginations a pattern which inevitably distorts the truth. Furthermore, in dealing with daily world events, it is simply not possible to present the whole truth and nothing but the truth in twenty-five minutes.

How certain can a jury be of 'the facts'?

Not all of us will be scientists or detectives but all of us encounter complex problems. Many of us will, at some time, have to undertake jury service. We might be faced with a torrent of facts about a murder; which of these would be most vital in forming a decision about the guilt of the defendant? We have seen that the evidence of eyewitnesses and even of cameras is unreliable; but if all the evidence pointed clearly in one direction, we might become certain. What else would be absolutely convincing? Surely the confession of the accused would remove all doubts. Yet there is at least one case in which an innocent man was executed after making a confession which he himself believed to be true. This was the famous Christie-Evans case (described by Ludovic Kennedy in *10 Rillington Place*) in which Evans believed that, while drunk, he had killed his wife and child. It was only after his execution that Christie was revealed as the real criminal; Christie had persuaded Evans to confess and subsequent interrogation by the police unwittingly convinced him that he was guilty.

The more facts we know, the less certain we feel about the truth. We would have to be absolutely certain about a man's guilt before deciding to execute him; hence the Christie-Evans case speeded the decision to abolish capital punishment in the U.K. At the time of writing, there has been a campaign to restore the death penalty, particularly for terrorists who kill innocent people with bombs. But are we any more certain now than we were a few decades ago of a person's guilt? And even if we could positively identify the terrorist who threw a bomb, have we established the complete truth? Are all the facts, including the names of all terrorists involved, known? What is the difference between this terrorism and war? Will the execution of one agent prevent further killing? The simple fact, that a person killed several people, is a mere part of a vast jigsaw puzzle of facts which form the entire picture. Isolating this fact may do little to help us see the picture as a whole, or to change it.

How our senses deceive us

But at least the camera will dispassionately record a simple event taking place in front of it. Our senses are not so reliable; we often see what we expect to see. Most people will read the sentence in the triangle as 'Paris in the Spring' (Figure 2−1) and, in a well-known demonstration in school science involving a glass flask filled with water and fitted with a bung and a long glass tube, children invariably fail to see an initial *fall* in the level of water in

FIGURE 2-1

Most people read this as 'Paris in the spring'.

the tube when the flask is heated (see Things to Do, p. 145). The author G. K. Chesterton used such 'blindness' in a story called 'The Invisible Man', about a murder in a small town; no one saw the murderer because, as a postman, he blended invisibly with the background of the familiar and expected.

The eye can be directly deceived by optical illusions. If we look at diagram A we can see it either as B or C and we can switch from B to C and back again (Figure 2–2). Sometimes we see what is literally not there; the 'doodle' seen in Figure 2–3 is composed of a few marks on a white surface, but the imaginations of many older

FIGURE 2-2

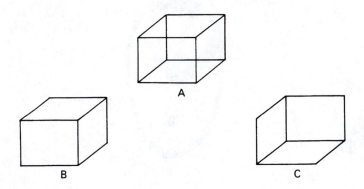

The Gestalt Effect
When we look at A we can see it as either B or C; often we are aware of only one possibility until we know what to look for.

people will supply detail to complete a sketch of Adolf Hitler.

Other senses can also be deceived. A man whose leg has been amputated can feel pain in his missing foot. Psychosomatic medicine deals with the interaction of physical and mental factors in illness; it reveals that patients who are convinced that they have a particular disease may develop the outward physical symptoms of that disease, even though they are perfectly healthy. More commonly, we are all aware of the human tendency to forget experiences which have been unpleasant, and to exaggerate — or even invent — those which were pleasant or wished for. This is no more dishonest than the formation of a complete picture from isolated scraps of information; we possess creative imaginations but we must learn to control them and to be critical of their creations.

The use of measurements in science

We begin to see why truth is rarely pure and never simple. The detective who works in the 'real' world may envy the scientist who chooses to investigate a small part of a complex problem in the seclusion of the laboratory. But even here, with efficient recording equipment and in the company of trained minds, there may be pitfalls.

Where possible, scientific observations are reinforced by precise

---

FIGURE 2-3

We often see more than we are actually shown
A mere squiggle? Or a man's face? In the 1940s most people would have instantly recognised Adolf Hitler; their imaginations filled in the missing details.

FIGURE 2-4

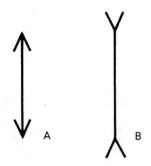

The value of measurement
Which is the longer line, A or B? Those who have not come across the question
before usually say B; those who are familiar with the questions will probably say
'both the same.' But it is impossible to be certain without measurement.

measurement. The line B (Figure 2–4) looks longer than A but,
if we are familiar with the illusion, we may say that the lines
are equally long. But it is impossible to be certain without some
form of measurement. We may be aware of the difficulties of
comparing lengths, weights, and volumes without being able to
measure them but we often overlook the possibility of error when
using an accurate instrument. Is the length of a piece of glass for a
window pane exactly 72 cm — not 71.9? And is the ruler with
which we measure reliable? If it is made of metal, for example, it
would measure differently on a freezing day compared with the
measurement on a very hot day. Small errors can be very important.
Even Shakespeare was aware of this; in *The Merchant of Venice*,
Shylock is legally entitled to a pound of his debtor's flesh but he
can see that, in practice, it is virtually impossible to remove exactly
this quantity, no more, no less.

Even in the most careful scientific measurements there is some
unavoidable uncertainty. Engineers allow for this in the 'tolerance'
they permit in specifications for sizes of engine parts. In effect, they
are admitting the possibility of human, or experimental, error.
Since this error is likely to result in a greater value as often as a
smaller, the average of many measurements will be more reliable
than just one. But the diagram (Figure 2–5) shows how the
estimation of a scientific 'constant' might require dozens, perhaps
hundreds of measurements; scientists persist with the refining of
their techniques until the results are approximately constant. Their

FIGURE 2-5

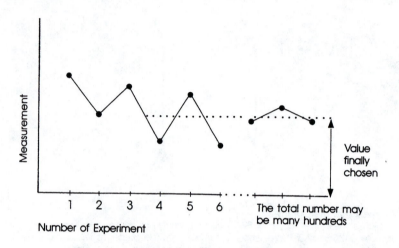

How a scientist estimates a 'constant'
The first values are unreliable because the scientist is improving his technique.
When the measures are approximately constant he will tentatively accept the
mean of the final figures.

final figure would be the average of the last few figures. Even then,
scientists will be aware that yet more refining of their methods of
measurement may expose hitherto undetected errors; like the rest
of us, they should beware of the attitude summed up in a famous
Groucho Marx quip: 'My mind is made up, so don't confuse me
with facts.'

In the light of all this, school science is often unrealistic. When
repeating a scientist's measurement, students have little time for
refinement and repetition; they may therefore be led to believe
that their 'good' results are due to good technique whereas they
may be due to good luck. They may also fail to appreciate that tiny
discrepancies in their measurements (which, in the circumstances,
may be attributed to experimental error) could indicate new, more
subtle problems. An example — the location of the image in a
mirror — is discussed in the chapter *Experiments*.

The very big and the very small
Some error is inevitable in any measurement and we must always
-assess it in relation to what is being measured. An error of one

millimetre is meaningless if we are measuring carpet; it would be unacceptable if we were choosing wire to thread through a tiny hole. At the seaside, the horizon seems straight, even to the most careful measurement. But from a high-flying aircraft over the vast expanse of the Pacific it shows a distinct curvature. And, back at the seaside, if we look at the horizon through a powerful telescope, it may — certainly during a gale — appear uneven (Figure 2—6).

Facts like 'the horizon is a straight line' take on different meanings when viewed through different frames of reference. In his book *The Blind Watchmaker*, Richard Dawkins accepts that the chances of life emerging by accident from primeval chaos on a planet like ours, just once in its several billion year existence, are only one in a billion. This makes it seem highly unlikely that life should ever have begun on Earth by chance. But consider the possibility against the full background of the universe. There are at least a billion billion planets on which it is estimated that life could emerge. Bearing all this in mind, the chances are that life could arise about a billion times in the universe. So why not on Earth?

Use and misuse of statistics

It is not easy to establish a single uncomplicated fact, and such facts are rare even in the unnaturally simplified world of the laboratory. It is easy to describe precisely what happens when a piece of pure sodium is added to pure water; in practice, even in laboratory practice, absolute purity is an impossibility and it is much more difficult to make exact descriptions when other, possibly active, constituents are involved. The increase in the number of these greatly increases the difficulty of observation; the final result may

FIGURE 2-6   **THE HORIZON**

...from Earth   ...from a spacecraft   ...through a telescope

Is the horizon horizontal?

be accurately measured but it is not easy to chart the course of the interaction or to know what is happening to any one constituent at any time.

For measurement in complicated situations the scientist makes use of statistics. There is a great deal of scepticism and misunderstanding about this branch of mathematics, possibly due to popular simplification of the information it supplies. A simple example is concerned with the tossing of a coin; statistics tells us that we will get 'heads' as often as 'tails' but we do not prove the statistical law wrong if we toss the coin six times and get 'heads' on four occasions. The 'fact,' as printed above, is not wrong; a better statement might read 'when we toss a coin we are likely to get "heads" as often as "tails."' The truth of the statement becomes more obvious the more often we toss the coin.

A more complicated example underlies the dangers in over-simplification. As a result of observations of many groups of young people over a lengthy period of time a psychologist might claim: 'Young persons growing up in overcrowded urban conditions, with bad housing and uncaring parents, are likely to be in trouble with the police before they reach the age of twenty'. The popular press might translate this into the headline: 'Science proves that poor homes breed teenage criminals'. The thoughtless reader's prejudices will be strengthened and the more thoughtful reader may even reject the distorted claim and overlook its potential value. It is this over-simplification which has given statistics—and sciences, like psychology, which make use of it—a bad name; it suggests accuracy and precision about individuals instead of a cautious uncertainty about groups of people.

Scientific laws

Having proceeded cautiously from small-scale investigation to a broader view; having taken care (especially when dealing with complex subjects like people) to be as objective as possible, and not record only what was expected to be observed; having repeated observations and measurements many times and had them checked by other scientists, the scientist will have produced a law. A scientific law is a broad statement of fact. Boyle's Law describes the behaviour of gas under pressure; Avogadro's Law relates the volume of a gas to the number of molecules of gas contained in this volume. Scientists use these laws as reliable bases for calculations and predictions—but they should do so with caution, even in a apparently uncomplicated cases.

Consider a simple law: 'water boils at 100°C.' As stated, the law is strictly untrue because it is incomplete. Water will boil at this temperature only if the atmospheric pressure is at a certain level; increase the pressure, as in a pressure cooker, and the boiling point rises. Again, the statement depends on the purity of the water; sea water boils at a higher temperature than rain water. The truth of the law depends on certain limitations; remove the limitations and the law becomes very hazy.

Unlike a law in society, the scientific law merely describes how matter behaves in certain conditions; it does not 'tell' matter what to do. We should not therefore expect the behaviour always to be predictable; the conditions may alter. Like a law in society, the simple statement of the scientific law must be surrounded by many conditions, limitations, and provisos—what we sometimes refer to as 'the small print.' Many of us have discovered the advantages of reading this 'small print' in legal literature, in guarantees, even in holiday brochures. The simple promise of the headline, *'A Mediterranean Cruise for only £400'* may be true—but only if we go in the middle of winter, pay extra for travelling to the port of embarkation, sleep in a small public dormitory aboard ship, and not eat. Scientists are aware of the importance of this 'small print' in their laws; unfortunately non-scientists often overlook it, to the detriment of the truth of the laws.

The detective may have thought that the scientist's task is straightforward; the scientist knows that the deeper we probe into the simplest of problems, the less straightforward the problem becomes. The search for solid, hard, unchangeable facts is bound to end in failure. All scientists hope to find, from a simplified laboratory investigation, is information which, cautiously used, will serve as a guide in the more confused world outside the laboratory. They will regard this information as they would a hastily drawn sketch-map when planning a route through unfamiliar country and they will not be surprised to find that these simple facts give only a rough idea of the real conditions.

Why we should be cautious in accepting 'facts'

We should now have a strong sympathy for our primitive ancestors as they began to take note of the world about them. It is difficult enough for a modern scientist or a detective to determine the facts of a particular problem; small wonder that thousands upon thousands of years elapsed before the simplest of scientific explanations for natural mysteries appeared. We had to learn—and are still learning—not to take any 'fact' for granted. Facts are all, to a greater or less extent, blurred by uncertainty. They may change, or appear to change, with circumstances. They may take on quite new meanings when other, hitherto unnoticed, facts appear. We may unwittingly invent some. We may also overlook others which do not comfortably fit into a pattern which we have already created. So we must learn to proceed with caution; to be constantly aware of our uncertainty; to be both self-critical and critical of the facts themselves. We may then be in a position to assess those patterns or to begin to look at new possibilities which will make sense of the facts on which we can still rely.

CHAPTER THREE

Fancies

Tell me what a man dreams and I will tell you what he is.
— *Carl Gustav Jung*

Sell your cleverness and buy bewilderment;
Cleverness is mere opinion, bewilderment is intuition.
— *Jalal-uddin Rumi*

Thought is only a flash between two long nights but this flash is everything.
— *J. H. Poincaré*

Basic research is when I am doing what I don't know I'm doing.
— *Werner von Braun*

It is the spirit of the age to believe that any fact, no matter how suspect, is superior to any imaginative exercise, no matter how true.
— *William James*

In science, the primary duty of ideas is to be useful and interesting even more than to be 'true'.
— *Wilfred Trotter*

Science is the great antidote to the poison of . . . superstition.
— *Adam Smith 1776*

Nominally a great age of scientific enquiry, ours has actually become an age of superstition about the infallibility of science, of almost mystical faith in its non-mystical methods.
— *Louis Kronenberger 1954*

The tendency has always been strong to believe that whatever received a name must be an entity or being, having an independent existence of its own. And if no real entity answering to the name could be found, men did not for that reason suppose that none existed, but imagined that it was something peculiarly abstruse and mysterious.
— *John Stuart Mill*

Sire, I have no need of that hypothesis.
— *P. S. Delaplace*

(on being asked why he excluded God from
his explanation of the Universe.)

Questions . . .

What *is* common sense?

Is it common sense to accept that we inhabit an Earth which is constantly spinning and hurtling through space?

What are myths?

How do myths differ from scientific theories?

Can we trust scientific theories more than myths? Why?

Since the Universe is so vast and old, is the scientific view of it any more reliable than the view of an insect, somewhere in St Paul's Cathedral, of the architecture and function of the cathedral?

Is God an explanation for natural mysteries, or merely a label for them?

What are parables?

Why do we read novels when they are not 'true'?

Imagination clearly plays a part in myth-making or the writing of fiction. Has it any part to play in science?

Is the model of the atom which we learn about in school science any more than a myth? If not, why not? If so, why so?

What is superstition?

Can we be superstitious about science?

Why do we believe in germs?

Why do we believe in psychological explanations of human behaviour? Are these ideas more reliable than parables?

Why is any theory better than no theory?

Fantasy helps us to make sense of the mysterious

A friend of mine (a woman who had long resisted the introduction into her country cottage of what she called 'fancy scientific inventions') told me about the advantages of her new central-heating boiler. In particular, she was delighted with the automatic time-switch which she described thus: 'It's marvellous. There's this little man in the system and he switches on the heat, keeps it at the right temperature, and then switches it off at whatever time I tell him.'

Though clearly not a scientist, the woman is highly intelligent and she could have, if she had wished, understood the function of the time-switch and the complexities of thermostatic devices. But she preferred to use the sort of language used by early observers to describe natural events like night and day. Indeed, although she knew something about modern astronomy, she might well have continued with that language in answering her children's questions. In a poetic mood, she might think of the moon as a modest goddess veiling herself with a cloud. Even in making such a simple statement as 'the sun rises at 0430 hours' she would know that, strictly scientifically, she was wrong, that the sun merely appears to rise because of the rotation of the earth.

Not only was she using 'untrue' language to simplify complex events, but she was also making use of a largely mysterious area of the brain which, having little to do with the routine and the practical, contains centres of memory, association of ideas, instinct, and imagery peculiar to the human species. And, in knowing that her statements are untrue, she may also serve to remind us that more modern, more sophisticated descriptions of events are also, more or less, mere approximations of the truth.

Origins of superstition

We have already speculated about primitive mid-winter rituals designed to placate imaginary gods who were apparently withdrawing light and heat from mankind. It must have gradually occurred to the more thoughtful of our early ancestors that, if they did nothing at all to appease the gods, the seasons might nevertheless continue in the same cycle. But human life, at the time, was short; history was merely the handing down of parents' limited experience to children. Very few would begin to appreciate that because a particular event comes after another, it does not follow that the second event is caused by the first. A man walks under a ladder and, shortly afterwards, is run over by a car; 'proof,' we may be told, 'that walking under ladders brings bad luck.' It is easy to recognize this as superstition and to explain it away by coincidence. But the more involved the sequence of events, the more difficult it is to distinguish a true pattern of cause and effect in stories created by the imagination.

The difficulty is increased by our discovery that even scientific facts are not as simple as they appear. For example, it is known that the use of a drug called thalidomide by pregnant women resulted in the birth of malformed babies. Do we infer that thalidomide causes such deformities? During the investigation of the tragedy it was pointed out that some of the women involved had produced normal children and the suggestion was put forward that the drug had prevented the body's tendency to reject a malformed foetus. The obvious assumptions about cause and effect could be too simplistic and could conceal the real truth; the drug may not have *caused* the malformations but may have saved the life of a foetus which was already malformed.

Obvious assumptions about cause and effect can therefore be over-simplified and can thus conceal the real truth. Although statistical evidence clearly indicates that smoking causes lung cancer, the exact chain of cause and effect is not clear. At one time smokers found consolation in a theory that those people prone to such cancer were highly strung and, since some highly strung people tend to smoke heavily, the simple explanation might be misleading. Once again we are reminded of the value of the warning: the fact that A is followed by B does not necessarily mean that A causes B.

Imagination should be controlled by criticism

People used to believe that mice originate in the fluffy dust which collects under furniture and which, when disturbed, moves quickly away — like a mouse. Imagination links the similar movements and initiates a superstition. But the idea does not *begin* as a superstition; it is simply a fanciful explanation (the scientist calls it an hypothesis) which, if accepted uncritically, *becomes* a superstition and inhibits further investigation. As we grow older, learning from our own experience as well as that of others, we replace old hypotheses with new ones. We learn to control our imagination with criticism. But it should only be control, not suppression; imagination, associated with a sense of wonder, is a quality which raises human beings above other animals. In its lowest form, it explains why we sometimes secretly prefer the fantastical to the more rational explanation. In its highest form, it accounts for the creation of works of art by the gifted few and for those inexplicable feelings of happiness which all of us suddenly experience, often by the contemplation of works of art, and which we describe as spiritual. It also helps to explain the sudden flash of insight which reveals a possible explanation to a problem; we sometimes call this inspiration.

Faced with superstition, we often suppress criticism. If we

believe that walking under ladders causes accidents we convince ourselves that we are safer walking around them, especially if we choose not to consider any accidents caused by the longer walk. If we want to believe the astrological forecasts in some periodicals we may unconsciously pick out from actual events those which happen to match the predictions. On the other hand, we may choose to look too critically at the predictions and dismiss them, without trial, as nonsense. There is a danger here; the rejection of an untested hypothesis may lead to scientific dogma. There may be more to astrology than horoscopes in daily newspapers. Following the tradition of Ptolemy, Kepler, and even Newton, a small number of modern 'scientific astrologers' have looked closely at masses of astrological data and found certain correlations between planetary positions and individual experience. It may seem improbable that these correlations exist but they stubbornly do; it may seem unlikely that they constitute examples of cause and effect but it would be equally wrong to dismiss them as mere coincidence or to welcome them as proof of the claims of astrology.

Pitfalls of 'common sense'

When we reject a bizarre explanation in favour of a more rational one we may believe that we are exercising 'common sense.' But we must remember that common sense varies with the century in which it is applied. If we try to free our minds of prejudice, of what we have been led to believe, and look at the daily movement of the sun, we discover a strong bond of sympathy with those who once believed the Earth to be flat. We need an adventurous imagination, not common sense, to see ourselves as minute specks of humanity clinging to an inanimate ball which is spinning and hurtling around the sun. Yet many of us believe this to be true only because we have been taught to do so; we have therefore no reason to scoff at more primitive people who accept the beliefs of witch doctors.

There used to exist in England a flourishing Flat Earth Society. The members were not all unthinking eccentrics with minds closed to new evidence and constant criticism; the majority supported the Society — whose beliefs included a saucer-like shape for the Earth, the conviction that recent pictures from the moon were media-produced fakes and that there was not such place as Australia — because they considered it healthy to challenge the teachings of science. At the present time there is an even greater need for this sort of scepticism. A scientist, however gifted, can be compared with a fly crawling on the inside wall of a cathedral; if it could draw what it sees, the fly's picture of the cathedral would be as crude as early maps of the world; if it could voice its speculations about the size, appearance, and purpose of the cathedral, the fly's opinions would be received even more guardedly. Yet theoretical physicists would have us believe that our infinitely large universe has evolved, in some twenty billion years, from a region of almost infinite density much smaller than an atom. Moreover they have plotted, micro-second by micro-second, the first movements of this process. None of us can check the accuracy of these speculations; but we do not have to believe them unreservedly. If we do blindly accept them we have simply replaced one superstition by another; the fact that the new belief has a scientific basis does not lessen the superstition.

Myths

Early explanations about the mysteries of the universe and about human behaviour became embedded in myths. A myth is strictly a part of a magical rite, an attempt to control nature by imitating it. Thus it was thought that rain could be caused by pouring water from pots and that winds could be created by waving fans. But such fictions gradually broadened to describe a great variety of natural phenomena. For example, the Babylonian Epic of Creation tells how the god Marduk formed the earth from watery chaos—a tale inspired by the constant silting up of the estuary where the River Nile meets the sea. The ancient Chinese idea of Yin and Yang attempts to explain differences in human behaviour in terms of the sun (the active masculine principle of life, or Yang) and of shadow (the passive feminine principle, or Yin) (Figure 3—1). Notice that the two are really inseparable, the existence of one pre-supposing the existence of the other.

Myths reflect unspoken, even undetected desires and yearnings and have always been associated with the urge to heal, both

FIGURE 3-1

mentally and physically. They appeal to spiritual hungers deep within the human personality whether they are expressed in time-honoured folk-tales or in modern equivalents like soap operas, tales of the Wild West, or Star Wars. These modern myths produce 'gods' such as John Wayne (who personified the simple pioneering virtues of those Americans who 'opened up' the West) or Elvis Presley who, through rock music, cystallized the spirit of restlessness and rebellion in the adolescents of the 1960s. There is little doubt that such modern mythology, despite a certain stunting effect on cultural progress, provides therapy for many unfulfilled individuals. The case of Elvis Presley is of special interest; some of his fans still cannot accept that he is dead. They see him as their ancestors saw gods of old, either immortal or capable of rising from the dead; doubtless, they find in him both a meaning for life and a comfort from growing fears of death.

The Beginnings of Religions

Myths gradually coalesced and evolved into religions and philosophies. Religions combined beliefs about the universe and its origins with codes of behaviour for their followers. Modern versions have certain elements in common but their differences ensure that they often remain isolated from, even antagonistic to, each other.

Many wars have been waged because of these differences and there is frequently strife within a religion because of differing interpretations of the central beliefs. Islam, the religion of the Muslims, has Allah as its deity. Allah is Power and Mercy but not necessarily Goodness or Love. But Christianity, whose God is Love, has inspired just as much warfare through the ages at times when its zealous followers tried to widen or maintain its influence. Other beliefs show less interest in the supernatural and more humanism; Confucianism in China emphatically claimed that the most important thing in life was good conduct (a view not unlike Christ's often ignored exhortation to 'love one another') while the Taoists insisted that the best policy in life was to forsake the world of action and live in harmony with the Principle of Nature.

The Greek approach to the mysteries of nature

Many of the differences between and within belief systems are often differences in the imagery and language in which the beliefs are developed and expressed. Such imagery originates from that area of the brain which is the still mysterious source of dreams and artistic creativity. By contrast, the part of the brain which is easiest to simulate by a computer is responsible for dealing with organization of ideas, logical problems, mathematics — what we call *reason*. The ability to question, weigh evidence, and argue was highly valued by the Ancient Greeks who developed reason as a superb mental tool. They distrusted the crudities of physical measuring instruments and believed that truth could be found by logic. Their counterpart nowadays would be those religious philosophers, referred to by Richard Dawkins in *The Blind Watchmakers*, who compare human life with an intricate watch and who deduce from this comparison the existence of a watchmaker.

One of the most influential figures in Greek philosophy was Plato (427–347 B.C.) who, being more interested in the world of ideas (the ideal world) than in the real world, encouraged the study of astronomy mainly by mathematics. The circle was regarded as the perfect geometrical shape and Greek astronomy depicted the universe as a series of concentric, crystalline (therefore invisible) spheres in which sun, moon, and planets were embedded and which had Earth as their centre. However quaint this picture may seem to us, it did explain how heavenly bodies moved without visible means of support. There were other Greek pictures of the universe which placed the sun at the centre but the one which stood the tests of time and mathematical measurements was Ptolemy's earth-centred model (about 150 A.D.). In varying forms it was to be accepted for the next fourteen centuries (Figure 3–2).

The need for myth in Greek thinking . . .

All this is not to suggest that the Greek mind was entirely and coldly rational. The Greeks, too, had gods but they were more down-to-earth and more obviously embodiments of human behaviour. The average Greek citizen, like the average person of today, probably preferred the entertainment of fantasy to the routine of everyday life. Plato himself, passionately devoted to mathematical, social, and political ideas, recognized the power of mythology. Much of his teaching is deliberately veiled in metaphor, in parable, for he admitted the undesirability, even the impossibility, of isolating rational thought from irrational fantasy; and he saw that abstract ideas might be successfully transmitted through fictions. He described sexual love, for example, as an attempt at a reunion, a re-creation of an ideal wholeness in human experience contrasted with the fragments of reality. Such imagery, to the Greeks, seemed the only way to describe and to begin to understand complicated natural mysteries. Philosophy and mythology were entangled in a way that seems as foreign to us as an attempt to describe scientific processes by poetry. We have made scientific progress by separating the

FIGURE 3-2

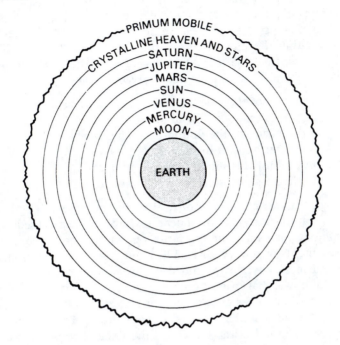

Ptolemy's view of the universe
The *primum mobile* provides the motion for the whole system.

reasoning part of the brain from the myth-making part. The Greeks, wanting to understand nature and not interfere with it, harmonized one part with the other.

. . . but myths have to be handled with care

In such an atmosphere ideas and imagination thrive. But it is possible, with hindsight, to see that the process can go too far and can lead to error. Unless the ideas it produces can be tested by experience no-one can know if the ideas are sound. In Ancient Greece, some two thousand years ago, there was no way in which the concept of the crystal spheres could be practically tested and this—and similar ideas—persisted and flourished. About 50 B.C., Pythagoras, the famous mathematician and mystic, noticed that harmonious notes could be plucked from a stretched string when the string was divided in simple mathematical ratios. (For example, if it were halved, the note emitted by the half would be an octave higher than that emitted by the whole string.) These ratios, Pythagoras observed, were the same as those of his estimations of the radii of the crystal spheres. He put the two ideas together and suggested that the motion of the spheres produced music which only the spiritually gifted were privileged to hear. Shakespeare refers to this belief in *The Merchant of Venice:*

> There's not the smallest orb which thou behold'st
> But in his motion like an angel sings,
> Still quiring to the young-eyed cherubims, —
> Such harmony is in immortal souls;
> But whilst this muddy vesture of decay
> Doth grossly close it in, we cannot hear it.

The idea was no more bizarre than the original conception of the crystal spheres. It may appear to have been accepted without serious question, but we must remember that astronomical measurements were very unreliable. Figures could be imaginatively stretched to fit any theory and it was tempting to believe in the reality of music that existed only in the vivid minds of those who considered themselves chosen to hear it. Nevertheless, the persistence of this idea underlines the growth of superstition that, for over one thousand years, succeeded the Greek age of reason.

The first atomic theory

Not all Greek scholarship was devoted to astronomy; other studies were, both literally and metaphorically, more down-to-earth. Around 444 B.C. Empedocles decided that all matter is made of four elements: air, fire, earth, and water in varying proportions; for example, he would think of the smelting of iron in terms of adding fire and air (the equivalent of our blast furnaces) to earth (iron ore). His ideas still linger; when we hear of intrepid sailors battling with the elements we must not assume that seamen have begun a study of advanced chemistry.

Around 420 B.C. Democritus introduced the first atomic theory. Each element, he said, was made up of tiny particles, the shape of which explained the behaviour of the element. The atom of fire was pointed and therefore caused pain, that of water was an icosahedron which rolled easily, but the atom of earth was cubical and so was relatively difficult to move (Figure 3–3).

Here again there is nothing wrong with the idea; it is simply too vague and impossible to confirm. But before we condemn the Greeks for accepting a theory without sufficient testing, let us consider our own ideas. We believe that there are about one

FIGURE 3-3   **Greek Atoms**

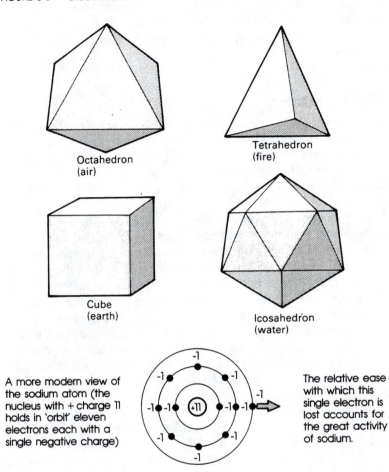

Octahedron
(air)

Tetrahedron
(fire)

Cube
(earth)

Icosahedron
(water)

A more modern view of the sodium atom (the nucleus with + charge 11 holds in 'orbit' eleven electrons each with a single negative charge)

The relative ease with which this single electron is lost accounts for the great activity of sodium.

hundred elements making up the millions of substances that we know, and we have constructed complex mental pictures of the various atoms to reflect the behaviour of the corresponding elements. We have followed exactly the same path as the Greeks except that we have modified, or even radically altered, the mental pictures to conform to fresh knowledge of chemical behaviour. The first modern atomic theory of John Dalton (from 1803) dealt with atoms as if they were miniature billiard balls, simple in structure compared with the models familiar to today's fourth formers, and even more different from the complex models needed for the deeper knowledge of the science undergraduate. We must never forget that this evolution of ideas about the atom matches progress in chemical knowledge; that the models are our own inventions; and that we shall never be able to see atoms or to find out, if they exist at all, how closely they resemble the creation of our imaginations.

Greek medicine

In medicine, too, modern ideas are different only in degree from those of the Greeks. When people are sick, they do not waste time in argument about the nature of sickness; they want immediate remedies. In making a choice, they do not want to hear theoretical discourses about the possible efficiency of a recommended cure; they look for one which has been found to work.

Hippocrates of Cos (460–380 B.C.) has been called 'the father of medicine' and his creed is embodied in the Hippocratic oath, a code of ethics still observed by modern doctors. It emphasizes the dedication of medical skills to comforting and healing the sick and reminds doctors to maintain a tactful silence about matters 'which ought not to be noised abroad.' Above all, it stresses the need for a strict moral code: 'Pure and holy will I keep my life and my art.' Hippocrates dealt with illness practically. Learning initially by observation and by trial and error, he meticulously recorded the results and, instead of theorizing about the nature of disease, used them to speed his patients' recovery. His methods can hardly be bettered today.

Some Greek hypotheses about the causes of illness may be primitive by our standards; they linked disease with vapours and evil spirits. But many of us nowadays look on medicine in almost the same way; germs and viruses may have replaced evil spirits but useful work can start from hypotheses which are later found to be pure fantasy. It has been said that 'any theory is better than no theory', because even a fanciful idea can initiate fruitful practical investigation. Thus, if you believe that disease is caused by evil spirits which inhabit faulty drains, you will try to get rid of the evil spirits by improving the drains. You will therefore succeed in conquering the disease; furthermore, if you have done so thoughtfully and critically, you may learn more about the real cause of the disease. But if you merely argue about the problem, or try to remove the evil spirits by prayer alone, you will not only be lucky to cure the disease but you will remain ignorant about its origin.

It was the thoughtful, methodical, and open-minded practice — not the vague theories — which distinguished Hippocratic medicine; and it was this successful practice that pointed the way to a more truthful understanding of the nature of disease. Unfortunately the way was impeded for many centuries because of the absence of reliable measuring instruments and of effective drugs. These would arrive only when the physical sciences began to take shape from the amorphous muddle of observation, rudimentary scientific thought, superstition, and mysticism which, with the benefit of hindsight, we can see in the relics of Greek science.

Aristotle

Aristotle (384–322 B.C.) was a pupil of Plato's but his approach to the study of nature was very different from that of his mentor. In the search for truth Plato recommended that we close our eyes and make mental images; Aristotle teaches us to open our eyes and look. He came to many conclusions which we now know to be wrong but he did so for the right reasons; he made careful observations, measurements, and calculations and he was well aware of the limitations of his technique, taking care to warn his successors not to take his discoveries for granted. In the third century before Christ he worked like a modern scientist. His chosen field was biology. He dissected and described in detail the anatomy of many animal species and his perceptive classifications were the basis of most biological teachings for the next two thousand years. He did not believe in evolution, as we understand the term, but he did write: 'Nature proceeds by little and little from things lifeless to animal life, so that it is impossible to determine the exact line of demarcation, nor on which side thereof an intermediate form should be. Thus, next after lifeless things in the upward scale, comes the plant .... Indeed, there is observed in plants a continuous scale of ascent towards the animal.' Then came octopuses, reptiles, fish, whales, mammals and, finally, humans.

The role of myth in science

According to Aristotle, what distinguishes animals from plants, higher animals (including humans) from lower, is the quality of *psyche* or 'soul' which they possess; the presence of this quality, he believed, was essential for life but it existed in different forms in various living things, man being most highly endowed and capable of achieving perfection because of it. Yet the *psyche* did not have a separate existence; it simply described that delicate balance of various bodily functions which results in maximum efficiency of physical and mental powers, an efficiency that seemed to be more than the sum of the separate parts. But many of Aristotle's successors regarded his poetical concept of the *psyche* more literally;

they thought of it as having actual physical presence instead of using it merely as a 'myth' to promote and clarify further investigation of what we now call psychology.

It has been said that the influence of Plato lives on because he left us with the great questions whereas Aristotle has been superseded because he sought to provide all the answers. This is unfair to Aristotle; he knew that his answers would not be the final answers—his successors assumed that the search for truth was finished. Not for the last time in history did a great man's disciples rest on the laurels that he had won.

Aristotle's influence in the Dark Ages

We see here part of the reason for the long stagnation of scientific ideas in the Dark Ages. A further cause may be found in the structure of society itself which reflected Aristotle's ideas about the natural world. He had believed that everything in the physical world possessed a 'nature' which explained its purpose. Thus, stones were earthy by nature, their natural state was rest and, if displaced, they tended to return to earth which was at the centre of the universe. By contrast, flames leapt upwards to try to reach the sphere of fire which kept the universe going. Just as everything in nature had its place, so members of society had theirs. Rulers, scholars, and priests occupied higher levels than labourers and slaves and it was unthinkable that the lower orders would ever rise to loftier positions.

This was an attractive idea to those in the 'higher spheres' and it is not surprising that the Church (the main focus of learning in the Western World) clung to Aristotelian ideas for as long as possible. Formal scientific study was directed to the verification by argument that God is the reason and the solution for all natural puzzles. Scholarship became a blend of Christian belief with the more mystical aspects of Greek thought; topics such as 'five reasons for the existence of God,' 'there is no soul or part of a soul in semen,' and 'angels were created after the rest of creation' were debated seriously and endlessly.

The religious/scientific dilemma

Such a system may—and does—produce philosophical work of great importance and intellectual influence but, by its very purpose, it stifles scientific investigation. The scientist who is convinced that the ultimate answer to a question is already known, will lose the scientific incentive and curiosity to probe ever more deeply. This dilemma (and it *is* a dilemma since many scientists of today have a religious faith) was recently highlighted by the suggestion that Muslims could benefit Western science. The Koran insists that we humans are all trustees of the natural world and, whereas Western science seems to have exploited and endangered our planet, Islamic science would proceed more cautiously or even retreat from policies which pose any threat. This is an admirable message and one that the West rejects at its peril; but it provokes two questions. First, it suggests that Western *science* is responsible for the threat to Earth; is not the misuse of technology, with all the political and economic links, the real threat? Second, the Koran, like the Bible, attributes the benefits from Earth to a creator; unless we teach ourselves to see God or Allah in a new way, more as a symbol of goodness, love, power than as a supernatural architect, are we not in danger of once again suppressing and distorting our hunger for truth in a way which helped to prolong the Dark Ages?

The alchemists' view of nature

Ironically, certain disciples of Aristotle in the Dark Ages pointed to another way. Aristotle had maintained the idea of four elements in nature — air, fire, earth, and water; these were the building materials for all substances and they corresponded with the four qualities, cold, heat, dryness, and moisture. They eventually became linked with the seasons and with human personalities; human nature was supposed to be a blend of the phlegmatic (associated with water and winter), the choleric (fire and summer), the sanguine (air and spring), and the melancholy (earth and autumn). The perfect person would be an ideal blend of these qualities; Shakespeare says of Brutus in *Julius Caesar*:

> *His life was gentle, and the elements*
> *So mixed in him that Nature might stand up,*
> *And say to all the world, "This was a man!"*

Alchemists spent centuries in the Dark Ages searching for a recipe to make gold which they regarded as the perfect blend of the four elements. Even a beginner in chemistry nowadays can see that the search was doomed. But it was not a complete waste of time; it resulted in the discovery of much incidental knowledge and in the refining of techniques which were to be of lasting value. But alchemy was not only a mixture of primitive chemistry and mysticism. It was also a philosophy of life which tried to understand human personality and spirituality as well as the constitution of matter. The search for the recipe for gold runs parallel with the search for psychological wholeness and spiritual harmony. It may be argued that chemistry made progress only when separated from areas of study which encouraged mysticism and, correspondingly, that personality problems would be better studied separately from physical science; but there are also dangers in such separation and the alchemists seemed to be aware of these. As Morris Berman has written; 'The view of nature which predominated in the West down to the eve of the Scientific Revolution was that of an enchanted world. Rocks, trees, rivers and clouds were all seen as wondrous and alive, and human beings felt at home in this environment. The cosmos, in short, was a place of *belonging* .... This type of consciousness ... involves merger, or identification, with one's surroundings, and bespeaks a psychic wholeness that has long since passed from the scene (Berman 1981). The alchemists were seeking to maintain or to restore this state of wholeness in which they would be more at home in the world and more at peace within themselves. They did so by elaborating the fictions which the Greeks had used to suggest subtle and intricate truths about human well-being because they felt that these truths could only be depicted in myths, stories, and parables.

The truths to be found in fiction

In our own scientific age we tend to dismiss the richness of mythology as mere fairy tales and we also undervalue the benefits of drama, fiction, and poetry. Aristotle did not see any distinction between the arts and the sciences; both nurtured the human mind in different and complementary ways. He included drama (which had absorbed much Greek mythology) in his studies of the natural world. We have much to learn from this attitude.

Shakespeare had no knowledge of the methods of psychoanalysis, yet his understanding of human nature is unparalleled; there have been more psychological studies of Hamlet than of any real person. The name of Cervantes' hero, Don Quixote, has moved into our language, his preference for an imaginary world of romance and chivalry expressing a longing that we all recognize. Although Tolstoy, Chekov, and George Eliot lived at a time when the methods of science were successfully exposing secrets of the human mind, there is nothing to indicate that their profound insight into human nature owes anything to the theories of psychology. Their stories and plays involve imaginary characters but it is arguable that their work, in common with that of other great authors, does more to increase our understanding of real people than case histories from a psychologist's notebook.

Mythology in modern psychology

This is not to belittle the great and influential work of psychologists like Sigmund Freud (1856–1939). Freud explored hidden depths of human personality and, like the Greeks, found that he could best describe his findings by using legends and folk-tales. For example, to explain perennial rivalries between young and old, in families as well as in society, he used the story of Oedipus who, banished from his home as a child in legendary Greece, grew up to kill his father and to marry his mother. Such stories—ancient legends and more modern fairy tales (like those of Hans Andersen and the brothers Grimm) which are based on folk-lore—do illuminate human behaviour but we must beware of dangers in applying them to our own experience. We must not, like Aristotle's successors, assume that they provide the only solutions to modern problems. Neither must we take them too literally or too accurately and see them as absolute truths. If we do, we transform them from suggestions into dogmatic superstition.

A disciple of Freud's, Carl Gustav Jung (1875–1961) considered that Freud himself had, to some extent, fallen into this trap. More than Freud, he appreciated the difficulty of describing, even in poetic terms, the shifting, misty, elusive world of the emotions. As we shall see, Jung attempted to emulate the alchemists in persuading us to listen to the messages of our dreams and fantasies, as well as to the symbolism of many forms of fiction.

Summary

As potential scientists, we cannot accept that supernatural causes are the already-fixed answers to our questions. If we do, we either give up the scientific search or we consider only the evidence which supports our prejudice. On the other hand, we must remember that scientific hypotheses themselves are essentially fictitious; they are devices, like the old myths, to help us cope with a truth that may be forever mysterious. And, most important of all, progress in science alone is no criterion of maturity either in society or in the individual human being. We are all emotional, spiritual beings who risk being unbalanced if this side of our nature is not heeded. So, in some way, we must consider the teachings of the alchemists and try to bring together two apparently divergent paths to understanding. But if we bear in mind that the devices for our guidance along those paths, the mythological and the scientific, are both fictitious and not literal truths, we may well find that there is actually only one path which, at any one time, we may see from one of two different viewpoints.

CHAPTER FOUR

Experiments

Aristotle could have avoided the mistake of thinking that women have fewer teeth than men by the simple device of asking Mrs. Aristotle to open her mouth.
— *Bertrand Russell*

Put off your imagination, as you put off your overcoat, when you enter the laboratory. But put it on again, as you put on your overcoat, when you leave.
— *Claude Bernard*

Nature gives up her secrets under torture.
— *Sir Francis Bacon*

In every useful experiment there must be some point of view, some anticipation of a principle to be established or rejected.
— *J. Gregory, 1772*

The experiment serves two purposes, often independent one from the other; it allows the observations of new facts, hitherto unsuspected or not yet well defined; and it determines whether a working hypothesis fits the world of observable facts.
— *R. J. Dubos*

The great tragedy of science — the slaying of a beautiful hypothesis by an ugly fact.
— *T. H. Huxley*

Experimentation is criticism.
— *Sir Peter Medawar*

No amount of experimentation can ever prove me right; a single experiment can prove me wrong.
— *Albert Einstein*

Questions . . .

What is an experiment? What does it tell us?

How do we choose between different hypotheses? By argument? By testing?

The ancient Greeks had many ideas on science which are similar to those of modern scientists. Why did Greek science stagnate and modern science make progress?

Galileo is often called 'the first modern scientist.' Why?

Can an experiment tell us the whole truth?

'There is no way in which a scientist can verify a theory.'
Why is this apparent weakness in science actually its greatest strength?

A spectator's view of experiment

Suppose you are watching a practical chemistry lesson through a laboratory window. The students are mixing small quantities of liquids in test tubes. They observe what happens or does not happen. They record their observations in notebooks. They seem to be engaged in some process of investigation — what happens if solution A is added to solution B? Are they simply confirming facts which are already known? Are they hoping to add new facts to their store of knowledge? Are they trying to find a pattern in the behaviour of the substances? Will they end up by discovering a new truth or scientific law?

This spectator's view of science is roughly that of the first philosopher of science, Sir Francis Bacon (1561–1626), and these questions were similar to those he asked himself. Bacon was not a scientist but he could see the power of experimental science in solving the mysteries of the natural world. He once wrote that 'nature freely yields her secrets when subjected to torture,' or what we now call experiment. He did not always see eye to eye with other experimentalists and he could not fully accept the theory of Copernicus, that the sun was the centre of the universe. But it was Bacon's views which first made thinking men take the new scientific ideas seriously. It was because of his enthusiasm that experimental science became fashionable. Meetings of learned men were set up to discuss the part it had to play in the increase of knowledge; one such group, governed not as in the past by the Church but by merchants concerned with the development of trades like brewing or bread-making, eventually became the Royal Society. Today the Royal Society is an important focus for scientific discussion as well as a centre for the administration of funds for scientific and technological research.

Science and technology

Notice the practical basis of the early Royal Society. Its aims were the understanding and improvement of skills which had hitherto been handed down by craftsmen from generation to generation. We see here the relationship between technology and science. By a dimly understood process of trial and error — a process which foreshadowed the role of experiment in science — skills such as agriculture, cooking, building, the extraction and working of metals were continually refined. Those workers who were best able to improve techniques were much in demand and some of these, curious about the reasons for the improvement, were stimulated to think in ways which we would now call scientific.

Originally, the Royal Society was primarily concerned with these skills which form the basis of 'the creative art' called technology. If today the main function of the Society is predominantly scientific this is because science, 'the inquiring art' seeks to understand and develop the skills. Sometimes it seems that scientific problems are very different from the technology that originally inspired them (the mathematical mysteries of thermodynamics are apparently far removed from the workings of a steam engine); yet we shall see that progress is fastest in both science and technology when the ideas from one and the practical experience from the other are combined.

The lingering influence of Ancient Greece

Up to the time of Francis Bacon, knowledge (scientific knowledge in particular) had been shaped by the legacy of the Ancient Greeks. Scholars of Bacon's time, like many of today, had been given a 'classical education' based on Greek ideas. We remember that Greek philosophers distrusted experiment; they preferred to develop ideas, even those about physical mysteries, by reason alone. They tended to belittle discoveries resulting from practical work, regarding them as crude compared with the excellence of their ideas. Even Archimedes (287−212 B.C.), the greatest mathematician and engineer of the ancient world, did not think highly of his practical achievements (a variety of mechanical and optical devices in addition to his studies of floating bodies) even after much of it was put to successful use in the defence of Syracuse against the Romans. Hero, about 100 A.D. invented a steam engine but its main use was either for entertainment or for tricks to sustain faith in religion — temple doors were made to open, as if by supernatural means, when a fire was lit on an altar.

This distrust of experiment was self-perpetuating. Greek measuring instruments were relatively primitive and admittedly crude compared with the Greek mind. The Greeks could *imagine* a straight line of definite length and no thickness but this was obviously impossible to draw; any practical model of an idea was therefore bound to be inferior to the idea itself. According to the Greeks, there was no useful purpose in improving practical methods for probing natural mysteries and so, as long as their techniques remained imperfect, any lessons from experiment could not be trusted.

Greek science did not make the spectacular advance that modern science has done; nor did it transform society on anything like the same scale. Yet Hero's steam engine was not remarkably inferior to the early version of James Watt's which started the Industrial Revolution. Could the reason for the stagnation of Greek science and technology be that each depends on the other?

The value of experiment

It is by experiment that we test our ideas, to find out if they work in practice or if they need modification; and it is by experiment that we often discover new ideas. Suppose we work out mathematically the distance of the image 'behind' a plane mirror. We find that it equals the distance of the object in front of the mirror. In making the calculation we assume that rays of light 'bounce off' the mirror at the same angle as they meet it. We can test this assumption by measuring object and image distances — if they are equal, our assumption about reflection must be right.

But when we make the measurements with an ordinary mirror we always find that the image distance is shorter by a few millimetres than the object distance. It is tempting to blame this discrepancy on the crudeness of our technique by calling it experimental error; and we may therefore be persuaded to assume that under ideal conditions the two distances would be the same. If we do so, we fail to make an important discovery about the effect of the clear glass which protects the reflecting surface; this glass brings the image nearer by roughly one-third of its thickness. If we were too easily satisfied with our experimental results we would not *discover* this.

Why Greek science failed to develop

Without the careful testing of ideas we might follow logical paths to wrong conclusions and overlook turnings to important new truths. This helps to explain why Greek science failed to make progress. Greek society separated philosophers from craftsmen who, obviously able to carry out specific instructions with great accuracy, were not expected to criticize existing ideas or to put forward new ones of their own. Without new ideas technology becomes stagnant and any scientific explanations which spring from it may, in the absence of practical criticism, be little more than fantasy.

We have seen that conditions were subtly different in Greek medicine. In the treatment of disease, whether or not the logical mind approved, experiment was of some importance; if a theory was sound, the patient got better—if it wasn't, he didn't. Thus the raw material of scientific method was present but progress was stunted not only by the absence of appropriate equipment but by a contemporary general indifference to experiment. It has been said that truth is like a tree, the shape of which is determined by the soil which feeds it, the winds which buffet it, and even the birds which peck at it. But Greek truth was like a marble column; it may have been lovingly and thoughtfully shaped by the artist, it may have been beautiful to look at and even useful, yet it was lifeless and unable to adapt to change. When progress did take place it was largely accidental and short-lived.

After the Greeks

For over a thousand years after the early progress of the Greeks, science was almost at a standstill. Principles devised by Greek scholars were still held in esteem by scholars. Too much so, in fact, because they were not subjected to the relentless criticism which might have refined and corrected them. These ideas, devised mainly by reason and conjecture but only partly, crudely, even accidentally, tested by experiment, were enshrined as truths. The limited progress which the Greeks had initiated seemed to have gone into reverse.

But here and there, in Constantinople, in China, especially where the legacy of Greece was preserved, there were signs that the scientific curiosity was still alive. A Byzantine mathematician used original views of mechanics to question Aristotle's teachings on motion. An Arabic natural philosopher discussed the possibility of biological evolution. Another, recognizing that hail originated in the upper atmosphere where fire was supposed to have its 'natural place,' suggested that if observation does not agree with theory it is the theory which is wrong. In China, alchemy had begun to develop

into chemistry and the preparation and purification of many substances were improved. One of these substances was gunpowder
which the Chinese used for fireworks; when it was exported to
Christian Europe it was used in warfare. Byzantine alchemy had
not made the same progress as the Chinese; nevertheless the
alchemists had concocted 'Greek fire' (a lethally flammable liquid
containing oil, bitumen, and saltpetre) which they used to shower
their Arabic enemies. Then, as now, part of Western science is
directed by the demands of war. The mainstream of European
scholarship, maintained by the Church, was towards the verification
of Greek thought and its combination with Christian belief. It
would have been in accordance with scientific thought to doubt,
even to challenge, the Church and to show that some of its beliefs
were wrong; but it would also have been heresy, a crime punish-
able by death. The most fundamental belief, and apparently
the one most immune to doubt, stemmed from Ptolemy (about
150 A.D.) who, with the help of much theoretical and some
primitive experimental evidence, had established that the Earth
was at the centre of the universe. This view prevailed until the
Middle Ages; it is encapsulated in the writings of Dante which
even show the exact geographical positions of heaven and hell
(Figure 4−1). Notice, too, the influence of the alchemists, the hint
that purification may be brought about by a retort-like device for
distillation.

We have already seen how social conditions in the Dark Ages
reflected Greek ideas about the cosmos. The Aristotelian natural
order which put the earthy peasant low down on the social scale,
with princes and priests in authority above him, seemed as invul-
nerable to criticism as the heavens themselves. But criticism did
appear and it began to grow. As a result of adventurous explorations
geographical horizons gradually widened. The economy of the old
feudal system was unable to adapt to the multiplication of new
sources of sugar, spices, wheat, and wood; sporadic peasant unrest
slowly coalesced into a class war. Faith in the old order was eroded
by new doubts; the common people began to feel that happiness
on Earth might be preferable to promised happiness in the hereafter;
learned men, admittedly in private, cautiously challenged long-
established creeds. The stage was being set for a new, emerging
science to contribute; this was the period historians call the
Renaissance.

Copernicus

The new science officially began with the publication in 1543, the
year of his death, of a book by Nicolaus Copernicus. For many

FIGURE 4-1

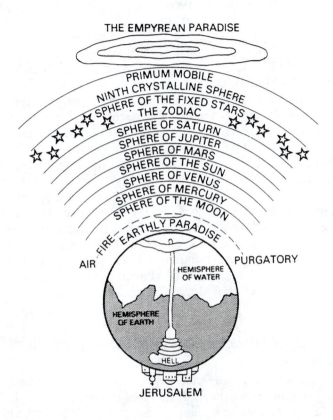

Dante's view of the world system (*circa* 1330 AD)
Compare this with Ptolemy's view of the universe. Notice the parallel with the devices of the alchemist, the suggestion that the soul is purified by a process comparable with distillation.

years before this, both within the Church and outside it, observations and measurements in astronomy had been growing in number and in accuracy. It was becoming impossible to fit the new data into the old model of the universe and, in a classic example of what would now be called lateral thinking, Copernicus had decided to consider the possibility that the model, not the evidence, was wrong. He devised a new model with the sun at the centre; in doing so, he adopted another Greek idea (by Aristarchus in 270 B.C.), but now he was able to support it with a wealth of mathematical evidence which did not match the old model.

His imagination—stimulated, he said, by the recent broadening of horizons on earth—must have warned him about possible social consequences of his theory in an age of unrest. As far as the Church was concerned he appreciated that his ideas were largely theoretical and likely to remain so; in fear of being condemned as a heretic he did not allow his book, *On the Revolutions of Celestial Orbs*, to be published until it could no longer do him any harm.

For almost a century after the death of Copernicus his ideas were questioned and examined and eventually his sun-centred view of the universe—modified by the latest astronomical measurements and calculations—was grudgingly accepted. Scholars within the Church received the new ideas with interest and with caution; officially they maintained their loyalty to the old theories. A sun-centred universe demanded a stretching of the imagination which they believed to be beyond the powers of most people. Besides, it displaced both humans and Earth from the centre of the universe. Our divine status, as well as the individual's place in the social scale, might be open to question if the new Copernican ideas were widespread. Times might be changing but the Church was determined that they should not change too quickly.

How changes in society accelerated the growth of the new science

However, despite any complacency in the Church, times *were* changing in more down-to-earth ways. With the decline of the old social order, cheap labour was not so readily available for agriculture; new machines such as watermills and windmills began to appear, and old tools like ploughs and horse-harnesses were improved for greater efficiency. At sea, the rudder and the magnetic compass were developed. The various European armies now had to cope with gunpowder and with the weapons which had been invented to use it. All this machinery demanded new skills which, in turn, made demands on the latent intelligence of those who supplied them. So a more thoughtful working-class began to appear, one which, unburdened by the prejudices of a classical education, slowly began to grasp—at least in rough empirical ways—the scientific principles underlying the use of the new tools. Thus an important link between thinkers and workers, a link which was missing in earlier societies, was forged. A new intellectual atmosphere, one in which science could flourish, was taking shape.

When this link has been made in research establishments or in industry, progress tends to accelerate, especially if the new ideas are seen to be potentially useful to society. At a time when explorers like Columbus were charting new waters, the demand for better navigational aids encouraged research into fluid dynamics and magnetism; in turn, the improved efficiency of ships and their compasses led to more adventurous exploration. Science, technology, trade, industry, the imagination of the ordinary citizen, all benefited.

The increased use of gunpowder in warfare is of special interest. The path of a projectile had long been explained by principles based on Aristotle's vision of 'the nature of things'; the normal state of any object was clearly rest, since moving objects in time 'naturally' stopped. According to this theory, a projectile, if fired at an angle to the Earth, would travel in a straight line for a time and then fall vertically to Earth. If this discontinuous path clashes with our own picture of a projectile's path we are either more sharply observant than the people of the Middle Ages or, like them, we see what we have been taught to see.

As a consequence of a series of experiments in which objects moved farther as impediments to their motion (friction, air resistance) were decreased, Galileo (1564–1642) challenged the Aristotelian view of motion in an example of lateral thought comparable with that of Copernicus. He turned the old idea of rest as 'natural state' upside-down; once a body was in motion, he said, it would perhaps continue to move forever in a straight line unless some force interfered with it. This would mean that the path of a cannon ball would be the result of two motions, one horizontal, the other vertical; the horizontal motion would be affected only by air resistance but the vertical, like that of a stone dropped from Pisa's Leaning Tower or of an apple falling from a tree, would soon be destroyed by the pull of the Earth. The effect of the two motions, Galileo calculated, would be a parabolic path—in accordance with careful observation.

No-one at the time could possibly have foreseen the far-reaching consequences of this combination of the mathematical ideas of Copernicus and the experimental methods of Galileo. Science was now firmly on its way to a revolutionary and comprehensive explanation of the universe which would have an incalculable influence on the roles people would choose to play in society.

Why Galileo was the first modern scientist

Galileo's contribution to science was not confined to the studies of bodies in motion. He developed initially simple investigations about pendulums and clocks, simple machines, thermometers, and lenses. First he observed their behaviour in well-designed experiments, then he constructed a precise mathematical description of this behaviour. Finally he extended a rudimentary theory to make predictions about heated air, projectiles, and even of the planets.

Subsequent observations and experiments confirmed these predictions. With his lenses he could see more closely and farther than people hitherto had been able to do, and he soon learned that things are not always what they seem to the naked eye. He became dissatisfied with the teaching methods of the day which concentrated on the uncritical absorption of classical ideas. He came to believe that the experimental, critical nature of science was a superior method of finding truth both in the natural world and in society.

The development of science is a two-way process. Theoretical ideas are tested by experiment, the tests show up weaknesses in the theory, the theory is reshaped, and the process continues as long as new and more careful observations are made. Those students in the chemistry lab were not merely stockpiling new information; they were, in effect, saying: 'If this substance is what I think it is, it will react in a certain way; if it is not what I think it is, it will react differently.' In fact, they were testing ideas. Notice that the ideas come first—from casual observation, from technology, from other investigations—and that they determine the experiment; the experiment then decides what ideas are wrong. By such a process the original theory may be whittled away, perhaps even abandoned, as a result of the experimental findings. Without suggestions from theory, experiment will, at best, provide new information which does not lead anywhere; without the correcting influence of experiment, pure theory may lead us away from the truth. But when experiment and theory combine in this two-way process, we begin to move confidently in the right direction. Ideas in Greek science were not usually developed in this manner and that is why Greek science is not what we mean by science today. Galileo's method of investigation made use of the process and that is why we call Galileo the first modern scientist.

Galileo's clash with the Church

Galileo believed that some of his experimental findings provided evidence for the Copernican model of the universe. He used a crudely assembled telescope to show that all heavenly bodies do not rotate around the earth. He was foolish enough to believe that this evidence would be quickly accepted. But officially the Church could only reject it; the evidence was supplied by an instrument which was little more than a simple toy while established theories were more than a thousand years old. However the Church had become divided; many of its scholars were on Galileo's side in recognizing that the Copernican theory explained the accumulating new data more satisfactorily. Yet they feared that it if became known that there was something fundamentally wrong in their picture of the universe—with mankind at the centre and God, somewhere 'out there,' in full control—they could no longer command the respect of ordinary people.

The situation was complicated by Galileo's personality. He had always been intolerant of people with whom he could not agree, and he had made enemies within the Church; he was also a passionate believer in spreading what he felt to be the truth. The Church, privately unable to reject his findings, suggested that its scholars could attempt to confirm and develop his work in secret while publicly maintaining the older views. Galileo could not agree and after much lengthy intrigue he was encouraged (as much by his enemies as by his friends) to publish his *Dialogue on the Two Chief World Systems*. This was a book for the general public, not only for the scholars of the Church, in which Copernican views were given much respect while those of the supporters of Ptolemy were ridiculed. The Church had to be seen to act and Galileo was forced by the Inquisition to recant. He went through the motions of recantation, was formally forbidden to produce more heresy but, as an old and respected man, was given only a nominal punishment. Even though he was publicly disgraced he was still able to continue his work in private.

It is sometimes argued by defenders of the medieval Church's repressive attitude to new scientific ideas that it was this critical evaluation by Church scholars which nurtured and encouraged the state of mind in which science could eventually flourish. They point to the turmoil of doubt within the Church at the time of the Reformation and attribute the rise of science to a harnessing of this doubt. But in considering the complex relationship between Renaissance, Reformation, and Scientific Revolution it is difficult to decide what is cause and what is effect; there were common causes for all three movements and each movement affected, and was affected by, the others. Many people feel that the scientific revolution was, on the whole, the most influential; in the words of Herbert Butterfield, 'the scientific revolution outshines everything since the rise of Christianity and reduces the Renaissance and the Reformation to the rank of mere episodes.'

Philosophical distrust of experimental science

Classical Greek philosophers had distrusted slave-associated experiment and, since the basis of education in Western schools has traditionally been the scholarship of Greece, it is perhaps not surprising that science, as a way of thought based on experiment, has always been regarded with suspicion in many philosophical circles.

We have seen that the first philosophical view of science was distorted; it presented science as Francis Bacon saw it, as a collection of experimentally discovered facts which gradually added up to a scientific truth. Galileo convinced future scientists that the function of experiment was to sort out possible ways to truth from the more unlikely. Yet because Bacon was a philosopher of great repute it was his support that helped to make the new science respectable, if still not clearly understood. Scholars continued to share Bacon's outsider's view, to regard science as an extension of Greek reasoning with practical methods of verification of its theories. Even today, in otherwise educated circles, this distorted view persists; it is not uncommon to read opinions about science from Cabinet ministers (including ministers of education) which confuse science with technology or logic and which equate the learning of science with the memorizing of technicalities. The idea that scientific thought is not merely a step towards great technological benefits but could indicate new paths to the solution of perennial world problems has not yet been universally appreciated by political or industrial leaders.

Since the first stirrings of the new science in the fifteenth century there has been one apparently insurmountable obstacle to its full acceptance as a way of thought comparable with Greek philosophy. Theories in science are based on practical experience and have been found to be of great practical use — but, grumble the philosophers, they cannot be verified. The sun has risen in the east for millions of years, but how do we know that it will not rise in the west tomorrow? If we cannot be certain of this, we cannot verify the statement, 'the sun rises in the east.' Such a statement is based on induction, that is, the more often B follows A, the *more likely* that it will happen again; most scientific theories are similarly based and we cannot therefore be *certain* of their truth. This doubt troubled philosophers for centuries; Hume (1711–1776) would not recognize the truth of theories built on induction — he pointed out that B may simply follow A, that there is no way of proving that it is caused by A.

In the meantime science went on from strength to strength. Most scientists ignored the philosophical criticisms, reminding themselves that, despite the objections, their theories clearly worked; their predictions matched the increasingly accurate observations of experiment. But the separation of science from the main stream of philosophy was unhealthy; the more thoughtful scientists knew that if a theory had flaws, sooner or later it would not work. Furthermore, if science were to aim at absolute truth, the doubts of people like Hume would have to be resolved.

Falsification, not verification, as a test for a theory

This philosophical problem has been much reduced by the work of Karl Popper (born 1902). Popper has shown clearly what scientists in the past have only hazily appreciated: that science can never hope to verify a theory but only to prove it wrong. If a theory cannot match observations, we know for certain that it is wrong; but, because we are examining it with the experience of a limited number of observations, we do not know if an alternative theory is completely right. The fact that the sun has risen millions of times in the east does not make it certain that it will always do so; the theory that the sun always rises in the east cannot be verified. But it can be falsified; if the sun ever did rise in the west, we would know for certain that the theory was wrong. According to Popper, any idea which can thus be falsified, which can be exposed to (and proved wrong by) the test of observational experience or by experiment is a *scientific* idea. As long as it survives such tests, as long as it works, the idea is useful to the scientist even though it may not be the complete truth.

All scientific theories are open to suspicion. They simply represent the best explanations of experimental evidence so far available. The Copernican view of the universe was better than Ptolemy's because it explained more fully the new astronomical evidence; we can say confidently that Ptolemy's view was wrong but we do not know if Copernicus' view is wholly right. Similarly we are confident that the theory of evolution is a better explanation of the facts of life than the book of Genesis; but this is not to say that the present views on evolution are the final answer to all problems about the development of life on earth.

Experiment makes the scientist's path to truth more, not absolutely, certain. 'The truth, the whole truth, and nothing but the truth' is an illusion; even if we found it, there would be no way of knowing that we had done so. As Karl Popper has said, 'In the history of science it is always the theory and not the experiment, always the idea and not the observation, which opens the way to new knowledge. I also believe that it is always the experiment which saves us from following a track that leads nowhere, which helps us out of the rut and which challenges us to find a new way.'

CHAPTER FIVE

Predictions

Science is nothing but trained and organized common sense.
— *T. H. Huxley*

It seems to us that it would be nearer to the truth to say that science is sharply contrasted with common sense.
— *J. J. Thomson*

Common sense is simply the collection of prejudices that the average person has made by the age of eighteen.
— *Albert Einstein*

Dogmatism has no place in science, and dogmatism about the unknown is particularly reprehensible . . . . Where knowledge is lacking we may extrapolate with due regard for the uncertainties arising from the incompleteness of our knowledge. The mystics too often neglect this caution. The naturalists must not . . . .
— *C. J. Herrick*

If scientists should not play God, they should stop trying to find God as well. The inquiry may be legitimate, but not as a part of science.
— *Stephen Jay Gould*

Although this may seem a paradox, all exact science is dominated by the idea of approximation. When a man tells you he knows the exact truth about anything, you are safe in inferring that he is an *inexact* man.
— *Bertrand Russell*

Darwin's theory is that, just as we learned skills like tool-making by a process of trial and error, so we learned which forms of behaviour had an in-built survivability factor.
— *Ray Billington*

I wished, by treating psychology like a natural science, to help her to become one.
— *William James*

Politics is not an exact science.
— *Bismarck*

This complete absence of philosophic doubt, this consciousness of superior knowledge through having received the revelation, are the hallmarks of doctrines which partake of the nature of religion. One cannot argue with its apostles, for, even when they appear reasonable, they will not be satisfied if one grants them their case in particular instances. One has to be prepared to swallow the whole lot!
— *Eric Toll (reviewing a book by M. and R. Friedman)*

Questions . . .

Can logic help us to look into the future? Can science?

If he were alive today, why would Sir Isaac Newton not be surprised at science's ability to put people on the moon?

But why couldn't *he* do it?

What *is* a science?

To what extent is each of these a science: mathematics? astronomy? meteorology? psychology?

Are some sciences more exact than others?

Scientific method

What *is* science? We speak of physics, biology, psychology as sciences but what is the common factor that distinguishes them from, say, history or stamp-collecting? We have the vague notion that science is more than the amassed knowledge about the universe that scientists have discovered and continue to use. It seems to be something more than logical reasoning, although scientists make use of such reasoning. It also involves the use of experiment which scientists use to check the results of their reasoning. Sir Peter Medawar (biologist and popularizer of science in books like *The Art of the Soluble*) seemed to evade the question when he stated that 'science is what scientists do,' but his answer focusses attention on the process of investigation; it emphasizes that the method of discovery of knowledge may be more generally important than the knowledge itself.

Scientists will often deny the existence of a single 'scientific method' but they will agree that there are common features to apparently different modes of scientific discovery. There certainly is no infallible sequence of steps for solving all problems; the nature of the problem will often determine the process of solution and only when the solution is revealed is it possible to look back and recognize a familiar sequence. Explorers make their way cautiously and erratically but, after much trial and error, are able to produce a sketch map of an unknown land which makes the expedition seem purposeful and relatively simple; the detective investigating a crime may be baffled by evidence which, when the puzzle is solved, is perfectly clear. This is why the only real training for a scientist is the solution of problems; learning how other scientists solved past problems will be of use only when he has experienced something of their initial confusion.

It is possible, in retrospect, to formulate scientific procedure, to provide the simple sketch-map after the explorer has done all the hard and often frustrating work. This may not help a scientist in a new exploration but it will indirectly illuminate some of the problems ahead.

Observation

First, the mystery itself. Casual observation may have located it and more careful observations, including measurement, will define it. Scientists will look for a pattern or rhythm in the events observed; for example, a doctor will ask the patient if certain symptoms occur regularly, spasmodically, or if they occur at all. Accumulating as much accurate information as possible, the doctor will also be wary of overlooking something which, apparently irrelevant at the time, may later turn out to be important.

Hypothesis

The next step is the development of an hypothesis. The very phrase suggests the logical synthesis of an idea from observations but an hypothesis may appear fully formed in the scientist's mind. A doctor, without being aware of the hints and indications gleaned from years of experience, may diagnose a patient's illness apparently spontaneously. It is at this stage that we see a similarity between the imagination of the scientist and that of the artist. The artist often thinks aimlessly, waiting for what has been called inspiration. It often comes when it's least expected; an idea may be sparked off by a chance remark or snatch of melody and the outline of an entire play or musical composition may come to vivid life. Various disconnected memories, scraps of past experience, have been floating in the artist's unconscious mind apparently waiting for some event to crystallize them in a new form.

So it frequently happens in science. Isaac Newton, sitting meditatively in a garden, did not solve the mysteries of gravity in a moment; he had already devoted much thought to the problems of planetary motion but it was when he saw the fall of an apple that he first conceived the monumental link between the two movements. Such moments of creative thought have been described as hunches, lateral thinking, acts of creation, as well as inspiration; they do not arrive on demand — indeed, they often appear during intervals of relaxation — but they usually follow periods of intensive, seemingly fruitless, research and they frequently bring together ideas which have no obvious relationship. The imaginative scientist therefore draws on experience from other activities; in early attempts to explain the behaviour of light, British scientists, traditionally interested in ball games, were generally associated with hypotheses involving moving particles; their European counterparts, more interested in abstract diversions like music, favoured theories concerning wave motion.

Experiment

Once an idea has been formed, it must be put to experimental test. The idea will have suggested certain possible consequences, and experiments are designed to find out if these will actually occur. The wise doctor does not assume that a first diagnosis is correct, but will use it to make certain predictions and then wait to see if these are confirmed. Some hypotheses are thus weeded out; they have been proved wrong or, as Karl Popper has put it, they have been falsified. Any hypothesis which survives the testing and which incorporates modifications which the tests have indicated becomes a theory. But the theory is not the whole truth; it is simply the least vulnerable hypothesis and it will continue to be modified and elaborated in the light of any new knowledge which fresh observation or experiment uncovers. Eventually, it may even have to be totally rejected.

This, then, is scientific method. It is what scientists do — or, rather, it is what they can be seen, with hindsight, to have done. In practice, the steps may follow a different order but the essential core of the process is the interrelationship between idea and practice, between theory and experiment, each finding new motivation from, each constantly stimulating, the other. It is certainly not a method of thought peculiar to scientists alone; history is not usually regarded as a science but if an historian tests an idea by searching for events which would follow from that idea, he or she is acting scientifically.

Prediction better based on science than on logic

The link between this two-way process of theory and experiment is prediction. The ability of a theory to make predictions which are confirmable by later events is a powerful support for the theory; the theory is acceptable if, in its ability to predict, it has not so far been proved wrong. If you can imagine something happening to prove the theory wrong—if it is falsifiable—it is scientifically respectable.

Logic alone, even the mathematical logic used by scientists, cannot predict with certainty. The precise and elegant processes of mathematics may lead to conclusions which are demonstrably wrong; they may make sense in the closed world of mathematics but they may relate only approximately to the real world. Mathematics, often called the language of science, enables scientists to form and develop new ideas but the ideas become part of scientific thought only when they have been successfully tested by comparison with what happens in the real world.

We are on even more dangerous ground when we leave the logic of mathematics and investigate the more common logic of everyday language. René Descartes, the French philosopher who did much to inaugurate the Age of Reason in the eighteenth century, was a brilliant thinker, particularly in mathematics. He was much impressed by the success of science but, like earlier Greek philosophers, he distrusted its reliance on practical methods. Much of his non-mathematical logic is invaluable as an aid to clear thinking but, without practical testing, it has led to error. For example, Descartes reasoned that the circulation of the blood was initiated by the heart which, he argued, heated the blood and caused it to rise, rather like the modern domestic hot-water system.

FIGURE 5-1

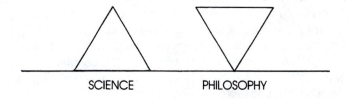

SCIENCE   PHILOSOPHY

To anyone prepared to do some simple experimental work with a thermometer, the explanation is obviously wrong; but in the absence of such practical testing the idea may persist because of the prestige of its creator. The difference between predictions made by scientific method and those by logic alone has been neatly summarized by analogy with two pyramids, one resting on its base, the other balanced on its tip (Figure 5–1). A theory developed by scientific method is like the first; it has been formed from a broad survey of ideas and evidence and gradually tapered by the experimental elimination of those which are demonstrably wrong. The result is a stable body of knowledge. On the other hand, a theory elaborated by logic may start from a single, attractive idea; it may accumulate other complementary ideas to become an impressive blend of cleverness and wisdom. But it is unstable; it may be toppled by a single, practical test.

Why astronomy is a science

If accurate prediction characterizes a science, we have only to consult our diaries to be persuaded that astronomy is a highly exact science. Predictions about sunrises and sunsets can be tested by simple observation; but these predictions have been made largely with the help of mathematics and we cannot perform experiments in astronomy as we can mix chemicals in a test tube. However, if we predict mathematically that an eclipse of the sun will occur at a certain time and then wait for that time to make the necessary observation, the observation itself becomes an experiment. Einstein's theory of relativity forecast that light is deflected when it passes near a large mass like the sun; normally such deflection cannot be seen but scientists took advantage of a solar eclipse in 1919 to confirm it. We cannot choose to manipulate the planets but if we choose a convenient time to make observations we fulfil the conditions of experiment.

It was, of course, Isaac Newton who successfully wove the findings of earlier astronomers like Copernicus and Galileo into the theory which is the basis of modern astronomy. The astronomer Edmund Halley (1656–1742), using Newton's theories, predicted that a certain comet would once more reappear in 1758; when it did, after the deaths of both Newton and Halley, it further strengthened confidence in their theories and became known as Halley's comet. Newton himself predicted the possibility of earth-orbiting satellites which we now use for communication purposes. In a famous 'thought experiment' he imagined cannon balls fired from a high mountain with increasing velocity. (Figure 5–2). The range of the first on the diagram is smallest; that of the second and

FIGURE 5-2

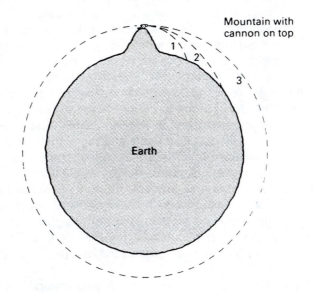

Mountain with cannon on top

Earth

Newton's 'thought experiment'
The dotted lines show the paths of cannon balls fired horizontally from a mountain top with increasing range. Eventually (3) the horizontal speed of the ball is such that, although it still falls toward the Earth, it never reaches it: it has become a satellite like the moon, continually orbiting the Earth and slowed up only by air resistance.

faster, longer. But the path of the third is such that, although the ball is falling towards Earth like the others, it never reaches it. It has become an object like the moon, or an artificial satellite, continually orbiting the earth and, being close to Earth, slowed up only by some air resistance and by random collision with tiny particles of matter.

The uncertain progress of chemistry as a science

If it is applied to a relatively small part of the universe, close to Earth, astronomy is a fairly simple science in that the number of moving bodies involved is small. Chemistry may be a less spectacular subject for scientific study but the number of substances possibly involved in an investigation is embarrassingly large. This fact, together with the mixture of 'recipes' and superstition which had accumulated during centuries of alchemy, partially explains why chemistry as a science was slow to emerge some 300 years ago. Consider the phlogiston theory, an example of an alchemically inspired theory, based on an ingenious idea and skilfully developed by logic and some dubious experiment. It held sway for over one hundred years before it was eroded by fresh scientific thought of the eighteenth century. It neatly emphasizes the truth expressed by that lone voice from the Dark Ages — 'when observation doesn't match theory, blame the theory' — as well as illustrating the tenacity of those who cling blindly to an old theory in face of new facts.

This theory attempted to explain combustion; when wood catches fire it emits spurts of flame and the phlogistonists assumed that wood contained much *phlogiston*, the essence of fire. When a substance had lost its phlogiston, the ash would not burn; if another substance did not contain any phlogiston, it could not burn. They predicted that the ash formed by burning metal could be restored to the original metal by replacing the lost phlogiston; so the metal ash was heated with charcoal (thought to be pure phlogiston because it burned easily away to apparently nothing) and the metal reappeared.

So far, so successful, even by Popper's standards. But the reasoning ignored vital evidence. Metals, when they burn or rust, actually gain weight and charcoal appears to burn to nothing only if we ignore an invisible gas which is heavier than the original charcoal. The alchemists did ignore such gases and, a century after Galileo had stressed the importance of reliable quantitative measurement, they even chose to ignore the increase in weight after burning. When Newton's successes made quantitative observations impossible to dismiss, some phlogistonists tried to explain the increased weight by introducing a quality called levity (as opposed to gravity) into the argument. Phlogiston, they suggested, increased levity and its loss meant an increase in weight. It was a fanciful idea — on the face of it, no more so than gravity itself — but there was a simpler explanation and science was already making it clear that there is no point in clinging to a complex theory if a simpler one will suffice.

It is probably obvious to most of us that combustion must involve the adding on, not the loss, of another substance. But this is being wise after the event, not only of the discovery of oxygen but of regarding invisible gases as substances which can be weighed like lumps of stone. It is difficult to imagine what we might have thought about the problem before Lavoisier (1743–1794) showed that air loses oxygen to the metal when the metal burns, and that exactly the same weight of oxygen may be restored when the ash is reduced back to the metal. Such explanations are always 'obvious' -when they are revealed. What is more surprising is that chemistry was still competing with the ghost of alchemy nearly one hundred years after the publication of Newton's *Principia* (1687).

The emergence of chemistry as a science had begun in 1661 with the publication of Boyle's *The Sceptical Chymist*. Although by our standards very much as alchemist, Boyle had begun to remove the mysticism from the Greek view of 'the elements' and defined a chemical element as a substance that could not be broken down into anything simpler. Subsequent progress was slow; even Newton viewed chemistry with a superstitious eye. Nevertheless he indirectly encouraged the new chemists to look more rationally at their subject even though it was not until after Lavoisier that the outline of modern chemistry appeared on the scientific landscape beside the already established shapes of astronomy and physics.

How Dalton's Atomic Theory helped to shape the new science

Once the foundations of a theory are laid the structure of science quickly takes shape. In the case of chemistry the scaffolding was the theory of John Dalton (1766–1844). The results of weighing the products of many chemical reactions had produced some interesting phenomena. For example, the weight of the element oxygen which a fixed weight of a given metal requires for complete combustion is always the same — 4 parts by weight of copper require 1 part of oxygen to burn to the black 'ash' we call black copper oxide. Moreover, when it is possible for a metal to burn to form a different oxide, not only are the new proportions fixed but the two different weights of metal which combine with the same weight of oxygen are related in a simple mathematical way. In red copper oxide the weights of copper to oxygen are always 8 to 1, and if we compare the black oxide (4:1) and the red oxide (8:1) we see that the weight of copper in the black oxide is exactly half that in the red.

This suggested to Dalton that elements like copper and oxyen are made up of tiny particles (atoms) with definite weights; in the above example, the copper atom must weigh four times as much as the oxygen atom and, when the elements combine, the numerical relationships are explained by the union of one atom of each oxide (black oxide) or two atoms of copper to one of oxygen (red oxide). Nowadays we write the formulae of the two oxides as CuO and Cu_2O. Notice that there are other possibilities which also explain the numerical relationship (the formula Cu_2O_2 for black copper oxide, the copper atom weighing four times as much as the oxyen, would also explain the experimental relationship of 4 parts by

weight of copper to 1 part of oxygen); but one atom of each
(CuO) is the *simplest* explanation and no practical evidence suggests
that it is not also the correct explanation. This concurs with the
ideas of William of Occam (Fig. 5−3) in the 14th C—admirable
advice for a scientist.

After Dalton, the conditions were right for the infant science of
chemistry to make rapid growth. It soon became possible for atomic
weights to be determined by a process of weighing, calculation,
and testing of various combinations of elements. Nearly two hundred
years were to pass before these weights could be measured more
directly (by the mass spectrometer) but, in the meantime, they
helped to make calculations in chemistry increasingly accurate and
predictions more certain. New elements were discovered and new
patterns of behaviour noticed. When all the known elements were
arranged in order of increasing atomic weight, the English chemist
Newlands (1838−1898) noticed that they showed a periodicity
similar to the notes on a musical scale; just as the note middle C is
'repeated' after an intervening seven notes by high C, so the
element potassium appeared as the eighth element after the chemi-
cally similar sodium. As a thoughtful, critical scientist he put forward
this Law of Octaves very tentatively but it was received with
derision.

About the same time in Russia, Mendeleev (1834−1907) had
noticed the same periodicity. By contrast with Newlands, he was
far-sighted and self-confident enough to appreciate that the list of
some sixty elements then known was not complete; so he left gaps
in his arrangement of the elements for the inclusion of those yet to
be discovered. Moreover, by consideration of the properties of the
elements surrounding each gap, he was able to predict the properties
of the missing elements. This made the search for the missing
elements easier; it is relatively simple to find a needle in a haystack

---

FIGURE 5-3

──── Occam's Razor ────
Not a physical tool, but a philosophical
device. Usually quoted as *"Entities are
not to be multiplied without necessity,"*
it is more usefully and accurately expressed as *"It is vain to do with more
what can be done with fewer".* In other
words, choose the simplest possible
explanation.

when we know the properties of what we are looking for. Eventually the gaps were filled and the new elements were found to match Mendeleev's predictions. Obviously such success further strengthened confidence in chemistry and also in the reliability of the framework of scientific method which had helped to build the new science.

Exact and less exact sciences

Although natural substances are usually impure, thus making predictions about their chemical behaviour virtually impossible, they can be purified artificially. This means that we can study the interaction of one or two substances rather than many and we can therefore be more certain about the outcome. In these circumstances we can claim that chemistry is an exact science comparable with the astronomy of a small section of the universe. Prediction becomes more difficult as the number of variables (substances, conditions of temperature, pressure, etc.) increases, and it is easy to see that meteorology, the science of weather forecasting, can be classified as a less exact science. To be fair to meteorology, it might be truer to say that all sciences are inexact but some are less inexact than others.

It is not surprising to find a sharp contrast between the predictability of chemistry and the unpredictability of the weather. The weather of the British Isles is affected by the multiplicity of atmospheric conditions in vast areas of the Atlantic and of Europe; but each of us is concerned about the desirability of rain for the garden within the next few hours, or about the possibility of a few hours' sunshine next Saturday for a village fête. We are tempted to grumble at the television weather forecasters when they seem to predict wrongly but, if we care to look at a map of Western Europe, we may be more sympathetic. It is easy to devise simple experiments that yield information about cooling, humidity, and condensation; we could construct a sealed container, like a miniature greenhouse, in which the 'weather' would be completely under our control. But laboratory experiments and miniature greenhouses cannot exactly match the huge variety of conditions over millions of square miles. This is why meteorology is concerned less with near certainties than with hazy probabilities.

The role of probability in scientific prediction

Many events in our lives are easily predictable — darkness comes at certain times, the sun rises at others; leaves wither in the autumn, new greenery replaces them in the spring. But we can never be absolutely certain about such predictions; their accuracy depends on atmospheric or seasonal conditions. Even very simple events could deceive us. If I let go of the pen I am holding, it will fall to the floor. Always? Would it do so in a spacecraft? When we begin to consider the number and changes of conditions surrounding any event our predictions become less reliable.

It is therefore surprising that predictions of some apparently random events are so accurate. We can forecast how many people will die on the roads of Britain on a particular Bank Holiday; advertising agents know in advance how many thousand copies of a magazine will be sold, or how many million people will watch a certain series on television; clothes buyers for department stores forecast the numbers of garments of various sizes they must order for each new season. These predictions, based on past experience and current trends, are highly reliable as long as conditions remain constant. If, for example, there happens to be a petrol shortage on a wet Bank Holiday the number of road accidents will be much smaller than the expected figure.

Yet the predictions can never be one hundred percent reliable. We may have to accept that a certain number of people will die each day in road accidents; but the figure may differ by one or two, we cannot be certain about exactly where the accidents will take place, and we do not know who will be killed. We can expect more accidents to take place on a busy motorway or that fast-driving motorcyclists are more vulnerable than pedestrians. But we cannot be certain about individual cases. Predictions of this type are based on the experience of thousands of former events; the more of these which are considered the more accurate the forecast. As we have already seen, we can never know whether a spinning coin will come down 'head' or 'tail'; we are dealing here with probabilities, with general trends, not individual happenings.

Is the theory of evolution scientific?

It should be fairly obvious that predictions in biology, the science of life, are much less precise than those in simple astronomy or chemistry. But modern techniques—particularly those involving computers—are able to deal with problems in a general, statistical way which would have been impossible even half a century ago. When Charles Darwin's *Origin of Species* first appeared in 1859, it initiated a rational explanation for much of the history of life on Earth. Since then, many evolutionists, having studied biological trends and probabilities and making liberal use of Occam's Razor, have convinced themselves that there is no need to involve any supernatural factor in this history. Anti-evolutionists have retorted that evolution can neither be verified nor (more importantly if it is to be treated seriously as a science) falsified; they insist that life must have been initiated by some divine spark and that subsequently it must have been divinely guided in a way that merely *seems* to be determined by chance.

But, about 1950, Stanley Miller showed that life could have started spontaneously. He re-created the primeval atmosphere in laboratory conditions by circulating a mixture of hydrogen, ammonia, and methane in a flask containing sterilized water. He then heated the flask and subjected it to flashes of high-voltage electricity to simulate lightning. After a week he was able to detect the presence of amino acids, constituents of proteins, in the flask. He inferred that, in millions of years of such chemical activity, the compounds which he was able to produce in a few days could multiply, become more complex, and yield a nucleic acid — the backbone of the DNA molecule and capable of replication. In other words, it seemed that life *could* originate by natural means. The weakness of the scientific case has always been this enormous time-scale for the development of a living species. In practice, the theory cannot be falsified if one has to wait for billions of years to test predictions. But the arrival of the computer has weakened this objection. In *The Blind Watchmaker*, Richard Dawkins casts doubt on the claim that the complexity of the human eye points to supernatural design just as the existence of a watch pre-supposes the existence of a watchmaker. He does so by simulating on a computer the interaction of the blind forces of physics with the need for adaptation to external circumstances throughout billions upon billions of years . Elegantly and convincingly, he shows that what seem like great improbabilities on an imaginable time scale become near certainties when we even dimly appreciate the enormity of the actual time involved.

Psychology as a science

The large number of influences on the shaping and functioning of the human mind make psychology as reliable — or unreliable — as meteorology. Psychologists' work may be concerned with individuals but they must base their predictions on the experience of many. Earlier in the book we saw how a cautious statement about the frequency of crime in overcrowded urban areas might be distorted by simplification to suggest that children from such areas are potential criminals. But even if more city children do, in fact, commit more crimes than village children it would be quite impossible to decide in advance which children will be guilty or how serious their crimes. To expect psychology to predict individual behaviour is equivalent to the belief that meteorology will tell us exactly what the weather will be like at noon tomorrow in Piccadilly Circus. Yet unthinking people often seem to expect this degree of accuracy from psychology because they believe it to be an exact science. Much unhappiness has resulted from these misinterpretations; for example, although it is true that Freud has shown that the suppression of many of our desires can lead to misery, he did not claim that giving free rein to our instincts and ignoring the restraints that civilization imposes upon us is a recipe for happiness. The fault here is not the psychologist's; it has its origin in a distorted view of science resulting from a disregard for the small print.

Danger of the self-fulfilling prophecy

Sometimes a prediction originating from such over-simplification seems to come true, but only because it is made to come true. Jean Piaget (b. 1896) studied the education of many hundreds of children and charted the stages of their intellectual development. He has made valuable contributions to our understanding of the learning processes of younger children but it is possible to be misguided by paraphrases of his teachings. For example, if he suggests that the average child cannot cope with a certain scientific idea before the age of eleven, some teachers may say: 'According to Piaget it is impossible to introduce this subject to ten year-olds' and may therefore delay its teaching for another year. So the children will not have the opportunity of considering the idea until the age of eleven and Piaget's 'rule' will seem to have been verified. If Piaget's suggestion had been used not as a rule but as a guide, some children might have benefited by considering the idea at the age of nine whereas others, of course, might still not be ready for it at thirteen. Like that of any psychologist, Piaget's work reflects what has been gained by the past experience of many cases; it suggests, but it does not dictate, what will happen to individuals in the future.

Non-sciences and pseudo-sciences

It was consideration of some theories in psychology that encouraged the young Karl Popper to establish his criteria for distinguishing sciences from non-sciences. He found that these theories were too vague and subjective for scientific use; in making use of Greek mythology and of terms like the Ego, the Super-Ego, and the Id they vividly describe human problems and provide stimuli for further study, but they cannot, like a proper scientific theory, be contradicted by experiment. Indeed, by careful and judicious interpretation of the predicted behaviour, the theories could be made to explain everything and Popper pointed out that this was precisely what was wrong with them. Yet such theories still have supporters who, presumably in the mistaken belief that what is not science must be nonsense, create a pseudo-science. In doing so, they tend to arouse suspicion about those areas of psychology which are truly scientific.

We cannot apply scientific yardsticks to the pleasure we get from the beauty of a sunset, the merits of a favourite novel, the relative values of recommended recipes for happiness, the shifting emphases of contemporary morals. The 'pursuit of happiness' in which we are all engaged involves activities which may be related to science, which may be investigated by scientific methods, which may even become sciences—but not yet.

Nevertheless, in examining these largely emotional issues, we must attempt to retain the critical attitude which scientific thought has developed. Many people, confused by the mysterious and terrifying view of the universe which science has helped to create, may turn for comfort and peace of mind to the belief in a powerful and benevolent God. But in doing so they may cease to question and to think critically; they may reject the findings of science because they do not appear to match their religious creeds. They may not accept that religion and science may be two different ways of thought, and that the truths to which each way leads may be subtly different.

Karl Popper has pointed out that many ideas such as belief in a God have no scientific basis; the statement, 'God exists somewhere in the universe,' *could* be true but there is no scientific way of proving it. 'Proofs' of God's existence are essentially subjective. They depend on what we mean by God; they may convince those who experience them and they may even incorporate some form of prediction. But the confirmation of the prediction will depend on individual interpretation of the evidence and sometimes on poetic (and scientifically imprecise) use of language. Scientific tests must be objective; they must not depend on the views of the person carrying them out.

Yet the fact that religious belief, literary taste, and moral standards cannot be scientifically measured is no reflection of their value; similarly the fact that science cannot adequately deal with these matters is no criticism of the power of science within its own sphere of influence. In this predominantly scientific age those who prefer the Biblical account of, say, the Virgin Birth or the Resurrection to a conventional view may appear prejudiced and reactionary.

But the scientific mind is equally narrow if it belittles the importance of the areas of human experience lying outside science. Ironically, in attempting to apply scientific method to spiritual or emotional problems, scientists have often behaved most unscientifically.

The need for caution in making scientific predictions

No science is absolutely exact. We can predict with great accuracy in astronomy and in chemistry, if we restrict our investigations to our own small corner of the universe or to simple, uncomplicated compounds. But with the complex chemistry of living matter, with the evolution of life itself, with the universe in its unimaginable entirety, we have to proceed with caution. The greater and more complex the problem, the less confidence we have in our predictions; but there is consolation in this. We have seen that the framework of falsifiability, prediction, and experiment is the scaffolding for the growth of a science; but we need not fully understand the nature of the constituent parts any more than a bricklayer needs to understand the reactions which make mortar set hard.

For example, we still do not understand gravity; the planets in their courses are pulled to the sun by invisible forces equivalent to the effect of enormously long and thick steel cables, yet we accept that there is truth in what superficially seems fantastic. But the accuracy in using this assumption, although high, is not perfect; Einstein was able to show that the great Newtonian synthesis of astronomy and physics is only a very good approximation of a more complicated theory—Newton's theories do not apply to very tiny or very vast distances. Einstein's 'improved' picture of gravity may avoid some of the difficulties of Newton's view but it introduces fresh ideas which are even more opposed to 'common sense' than invisible forces. Yet, since these ideas make scientific sense in their capacity to predict events, we must temporarily accept them. At the same time we must remind ourselves that our imaginations are moulded by the three-dimensional world around us and, like the post-Copernicans, we must constantly strive to stretch these imaginations. It may be that, in the modern scientific world, we have stretched them to the limit, that we can understand new developments in science only by comparisons or analogies; like the Greeks we may have to depend on myths for some vague understanding of the whole truth. It is here that we have to exercise the greatest care.

We must accept these myths, these analogies, as guides and not as scientific certainties; otherwise we transform an evolving and imperfect science into an inert mass of dogma and superstition.

In adopting the caution and the humility of the true scientist we can move confidently in the right direction, but towards a truth that we may never be able to see in its entirety.

CHAPTER SIX

Models

The edifice of science not only requires material, but also a plan. Without the material, the plan alone is but a castle in the air—a mere possibility; whilst the material without a plan is but useless matter.
— *D. I. Mendeléev*

Many scientific theories have, for very long periods of time, stood the test of experience until they had to be discarded owing to man's decision, not merely to make other experiments, but to have different experiences.
— *E. Heller*

False views . . . do very little harm, for everyone takes a salutary pleasure in proving their falseness; and when this is done, one path towards error is closed and the road to truth is often at the same time opened.
— *Charles Darwin*

Truth in science can be defined as the working hypothesis best suited to open the way to the next better one.
— *Konrad Lorenz*

To him who is a discoverer in this field, the products of his imagination appear so necessary and natural that he regards them, and would like to have others regard them, not as creations of thought but as given realities.
— *Albert Einstein*

These things—the beauty, the memory of our past—are good images of what we really desire; but if they are mistaken for the thing itself they turn into dumb idols, breaking the hearts of their worshippers.
— *C. S. Lewis*

Science commits suicide when it adopts a creed.
— *T. H. Huxley*

I plead for the casting aside of all models and for the wholesale employment of mathematical formulae in their stead, because the latter are found more suitable for the representation of ultimate physical reality.
— *Edwin Schrödinger*

Questions . . .

What is meant by a scientific model?

What is a paradigm?

It can be proved that the three angles of a triangle add up to 180°. In what circumstances is this proof misleading? Is it therefore wrong?

'Ptolemy's model of the universe became a cage from which Copernicus had to escape.' Has the Copernican model become a cage for us? How can we escape?

'The world of economics needs a Copernicus.' What does this mean?

What is a model?

When an enthusiastic sports commentator refers to an athlete as 'lion-hearted' it is not being suggested that the athlete is some biological freak. The commentator is trying, with the help of a metaphor, to convey his or her impressions of the athlete's strength and tenacity. The athlete might have been described as possessing qualities that are like those of a lion, or are reminiscent of a lion. But this actual description, a sort of verbal shorthand, is more pungent.

We all make use of such devices when we try to describe the invisible, the abstract, the complex, the mysterious, and not only in language. We construct convoluted schemes of traffic flow to enable us speedily to negotiate the warren of streets in our cities; but the direction signs are not always geographically true. We may be directed to turn right for our destination when we know that the destination lies to the left; but we follow the rules of the scheme and eventually arrive. We accept that the scheme is not reality but a simplified representation of reality, or a model.

One of the best examples of such models is the map of London's subway system, the Underground. This is certainly not a true picture of the system; the heavily used centre section is expanded, the suburbs are squeezed. The routes are shown to be straight when, in reality, they twist and turn. Clarity, not geographical truth, is the keynote; the map allows the visitor to London to move with confidence from one area to another. A more 'truthful' map, like an ordnance survey map, would almost certainly make the visitor lose his or her way.

To the regular London Underground traveller, the names St.

Paul's, Piccadilly, Wimbledon, Wembley conjure different mental pictures from those experienced by bus travellers. And, depending on individual interests, all travellers may have personal mental maps of London. That of the book lover will highlight the location of the best book shops, whereas that of the theatregoer may have theatres as landmarks. All these maps are guides to different personal 'worlds' within one communal world; each has its own individual meaning, unfamiliar and useless to anyone else, but a guide, even a comfort, to its owner.

What we, in effect, are saying when we use one of these models, or live in one of these worlds, is: 'let us proceed *as if* life (or the local geography, or the problem) were as simple as the model suggests'. Then, if we arrive safely at where we were aiming, the model has served its purpose; if it ever lets us down, we shall either have to modify it or abandon it for one that is more reliable. We have seen examples from history—the Greek myths, the idea of the crystal spheres, Aristotle's ladder of creation; and, even though Aristotle himself did not do so, we are not necessarily wrong to speak of imaginary qualities like the *psyche* or soul as having actual existence if it helps us to understand some of the complex behaviour of human beings. But we must always be aware of the danger of assuming that they are real. Greek astrologers imagined similarities between patterns of planets in the universe (the macrocosm) and the 'humours' that accounted for the behaviour of the human body (the microcosm). In a pre-scientific era their ideas motivated useful investigation in both astronomy and medicine but we would be foolish to be guided by these ideas today. If we use them at all, it will be in a limited, poetical sense.

Models in religion

Such astrological fantasies may now have been exposed by the searching light of science as literally untrue but we must not forget that they may have a function in suggesting some order and meaning in a confused reality. The various religions of the world have similarly satisfied this hunger for understanding. Faced with the puzzle of creation and the often erratic behaviour of nature, our ancestors crystallized their fear and wonder in supernatural explanations. In order to find some unifying and supporting presence in an otherwise bewildering chaos, the early Greeks imagined that the entire universe was supported on the shoulders of one of their gods called Atlas; in Ancient Egypt, where the Nile provided miraculous life-giving benefits in the surrounding desert, Osiris was a river god who knew all the secrets of agriculture; but similarly

peaceful vegetation deities in India were gradually replaced, after
Aryan invasion, by more aggressive gods who rode into battle in
fiery chariots and used the energy of thunderstorms as weapons.
Jehovah, a later god of Israel, was believed to be the one and only
God responsible for the entire world and its behaviour; through
the Jews, all the people of the world would come under his (not
always benevolent), care and guidance.

In time, most religions have evolved in the direction of one
god or, in the case of the Eastern religions, of a few philosophical
principles. Gautama (born about the sixth century B.C.), the founder
of Buddhism, became dissatisfied with belief in many gods; he
planned a new framework of thought which would involve everyone, not only priests, monks, and nuns. The aim was a completely
happy state of mind in which the believer ceased to worry about
the unhappy present or the uncertain future; kindness to one's
fellows and high moral standards were essential to the process.
Buddhism spread farther east to China where for a long time it
replaced Confucianism and Taoism, which had also begun to preach
less about their particular gods and more about human relationships.
Confucianism served as a guide in everyday living; Taoism added a
flavour of the irrational; while Buddhism was appropriate for fu-
nerals and the hereafter. The Chinese therefore seemed to have the
best of all possible worlds.

Even though there was obviously nothing supernatural about
Gautama in India or Confucius in China, their teachings inspired
such wonder that many of their disciples attributed to them supernatural origins. Divine parentage and virgin births are ideas which
are not confined to Christianity alone. These myths are understandable when we remember that they arose from popular folk
tales which tried to convey to largely illiterate people, in images
which they could grasp, the marvels of the preachers' messages.
The story of Christ involves many incidents which may only metaphorically be true but we need not reject it as totally false because
of these elaborations. Even if the life of Christ, like the lives of
some other prophets, could be shown to be complete fiction, Christ's
view of human experience — the Christian model of the world —
can be of incalculable value in our various relationships and in our
control of our own behaviour.

Most of us, certainly in the Western World, find it easier to
think of human relationships not in abstract theories but in familiar,
even in family situations. It is therefore not surprising that many
religions deliver their messages in terms of a 'heavenly father' or a
'mother goddess' or divine and all-powerful leaders. We appreciate
the roles of such beings by comparison with our own families and
communities. Knowing the shortcomings of these human groups

we can also begin to imagine a better world in which these short-comings would have disappeared, in which life would proceed happily and peacefully as long as its inhabitants obeyed its rules. Then, if we wish, we can strive to create such a world.

Some Eastern thinkers, on the other hand, have gradually abandoned such models and they have often been accused of being too vague and abstract. But in moving away from concrete imagery to contemplation, in concentrating more on the individual than on the community, they may have decided that our models, like the myths of ancient times, are too rigid and impossible to realise; perhaps it is easier to bring about changes in ourselves than to change the world. Thus, some of their teachings may seem to us to encourage acceptance of social evils to the point of apathy, but they certainly embody much wisdom in persuading us to make the best of what we have got.

Western ways of thought have been influenced by the success of modern science but it may be that, if we wish to live richer, fuller, and more balanced lives, we have much to learn from the East. If we do, we may yet again be conforming to the latest trends in science. Contemporary physicists have found that they have much in common with Eastern mystics; in the dynamic world of the 'new' physics there is no place for static models or solid particles, even for 'reality' as we think of it. This exactly coincides with the Buddhist view of experience, in terms of time, movement, and transformation. Reality, according to Fritjof Capra, the physicist author of *The Tao of Physics*, lies not in substance but in relationships.

How we adjust to different worlds

As we go through different experiences in our everyday lives we create our own worlds and learn to adjust responses in moving from one to another. The scene on a theatre stage may, in the words of a once popular song, be 'only a paper moon, shining over a cardboard sea' but part of our minds translates it into a romantic setting which we can inhabit in imagination. After the play is over, we do not experience a shock if we see an actor, who moved us to tears in a death scene, alive and well in the pub around the corner. Coleridge (1772–1834) called the adjustment 'that willing suspension of disbelief' and he equated it with 'poetic faith.' According to him we see our experiences reflected in the work of the poet or dramatist and we are then inspired to make a purposeful mental pattern of these experiences. And not only while we are watching a play or reading; like the hero of James Thurber's story, *The Secret Life of Walter Mitty*, we continually create our own reassuring worlds of illusion which provide both understanding and comfort—up to a point. There is an old joke about a neurotic being a person who makes castles in the air, a psychotic who actually lives in them, and the psychiatrist who collects the rent. We are all neurotics but we must beware of becoming psychotics.

Coleridge described the pattern-building function of the imagination as 'the true inward creatrix' which 'out of the chaos of elements or shattered fragments of memory put together some form to fit it.' He could have been writing either about patterns of poetry or of science for he lived at a time when a poet and philosopher like himself could influence scientists; he himself stimulated Humphrey Davy to seek an underlying unity of the various manifestations of physical force—electric, magnetic, and gravitational. The Greeks, of course, looked on their studies of man and nature as the same investigation; their theatres can be seen as a model of the universe with man on the stage at the centre. In sixteenth century Padua the Anatomy Theatre (Figure 6–1), built to a similar design, had a human corpse at the centre for the demonstration of dissection; thus the spirit of man and man's anatomy were studied on similar stages. But just as modern science has removed the human species from the centre of the universe, just as many modern musical plays are more concerned with the

FIGURE 6-1   **Two Theatres For The Study Of Mankind**

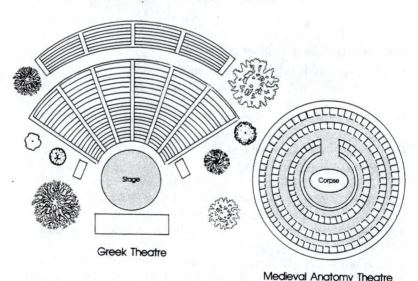

Greek Theatre

Medieval Anatomy Theatre

technology of mobile scenery than with human emotions, so modern studies of human problems too often see their subject as a mere mechanical or statistical figure. We no longer see drama and science as similar studies; perhaps both the problems and the investigations would benefit if we did.

How 'real' is the world of science?

Because of its success in dealing with the mysteries of nature we may be tempted to think of the scientific world as more truthful, more in contact with reality than the world of drama or of poetry. Yet the scientific world is created from assemblies of theoretical models which, like the London Underground map, enable scientists to negotiate with confidence a complex system of ideas. Every scientific model makes sense of current information and views on its subject but, with new information, it may eventually have to be replaced. If anyone had chosen to stick to the old crystal sphere model of the universe the flight of the first space rocket would have shattered those ideas. All models that scientists use to understand natural mysteries from atoms to galaxies are artificially made, and therefore illusory. But, within their limits, they work.

Even the flat, two-dimensional world of Euclidean geometry has its uses; as long as we are able to assume (as we are in normal circumstances) that the Earth is flat, we could build skyscrapers by the sea, having first viewed the horizon and established the line perpendicular to this as the vertical. We could navigate relatively large areas of ocean using the same system of geometry, although we might begin to notice errors in our calculations as we ventured farther. In the world of Euclidean geometry the angles of a triangle add up to 180°; there can be only right angle in a Euclidean triangle. But, if we were to make a straight line between two points at a large distance apart on the Pacific Ocean and make two further straight lines, one at each end, perpendicular to the first, these two lines would meet at the North Pole; we would have constructed a triangle with two right angles. The Euclidean two-dimensional world and the real world no longer match.

The fact that we know that the real world is approximately a sphere does not mean that we completely reject Euclidean geometry. Newton's model of the universe was not discarded when Einstein showed that the older model had its limits; we still use Newton's laws to put men on the moon, to solve a multitude of mundane engineering problems, or — often without conscious effort — to adjust our walking or driving, flying or sailing, to changing atmospheric or geographic conditions. For routine calculations in chemistry we

FIGURE 6-2

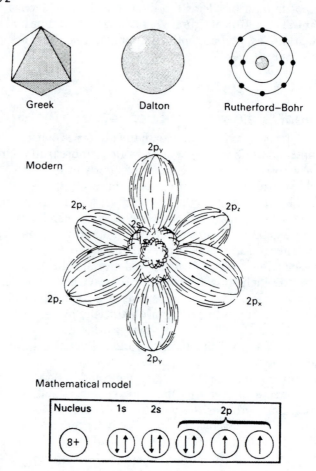

Greek   Dalton   Rutherford–Bohr

Modern

Mathematical model

Models of the oxygen atom
The atom is impossible to visualise and is more usefully depicted mathematically.

may still think of atoms as small billiard balls with different weights for different elements; for more complicated problems involving the union of elements, we find it convenient to regard atoms as mini solar systems; and for investigations of the huge energy potential in matter, we must consider models of the atom which are more mathematical than pictorial (Figure 6–2). None of these models is useless because it is essentially illusory; each serves its purpose of clarifying problems at different levels of difficulty; each has contributed to progress in understanding and to making use of the principles of chemistry and atomic physics.

How models help the scientist

Scientific investigation begins when an intellectual model, however primitive, replaces some of the veils of mysticism which have hitherto surrounded a problem. The way ahead now seems a little clearer. Aristotle's work in biology was guided by the idea of similarity between parent and offspring, so he was led to believe that species of animals and plants were unchangeable. But there are tiny differences which Aristotle overlooked and which, later, could not be contained by his model. It was to make sense of these that Darwin devised a new model; he called it Natural Selection by comparison with the artificial selection which a breeder makes in aiming at qualities he wants in a plant or animal. The new model, having dispensed with the mystery of the old, now began to develop as it progressively explained what might formerly have been attributed to the supernatural.

It seems that scientists have first to be convinced that mysteries are capable of being investigated by rational means. Then a model can be created and allowed to develop. But when the model can no longer explain fresh mysteries, there is again the temptation to cling to it and assume that the new phenomena are supernatural. In the 1960s Jacques Monod asserted that all living things evolved by chance and necessity alone, that there was no longer any need to bring the supernatural into consideration of biological problems. But some phenomena have remained strangely resistant to rational explanation. Arthur Koestler discussed some of these in his book, *The Ghost in the Machine*. Some birds for example, emerge from their shells apparently already programmed to detect dangers which, in the past, they were assumed to avoid by experience; most children succeed uncannily well in the familiar but extraordinarily complex task of learning to speak. The 'illusions' of a mind separate from the body, of plan and purpose in the evolutionary process, are so insistent that the pressure to accept the idea of a 'ghost' in the machine' becomes almost irresistible. In these circumstances it must not be forgotten that a truly scientific investigation does not rule out the possibility of a 'ghost'; but we must also remember that too early acceptance of supernatural beliefs will stop all scientific progress. We must continue to assume that all mysteries are explorable by scientific method; as Jonathan Miller has put it, we must persist in looking for 'a machine within the ghost.'

When does a model have to be replaced?

When a machine, or model, gets bogged down in new mysteries it has to be replaced. Newton found it convenient to regard light as a stream of tiny particles but this idea could not explain the mutual interference of two rays of light nor, eventually, could it account for the difference in speeds of light in different media. So a new model, of light as wave motion, was established (Figure 6–3). In its turn, the wave theory of radiation ran into difficulties; in certain experiments streams of electrons (which produce light in our television screens) behave like bullets from a machine-gun, in others they show a wave-like quality. When Lord Rutherford was asked for his views on this dual nature, he replied: 'On Mondays, Wednesdays, and Fridays I think of electrons as particles, but on Tuesdays, Thursdays, and Saturdays I think of them as waves.'

This was the proper scientific attitude to models — as devices selected for specific purposes; working with one model demands obedience to its internal laws and conditions and automatically shuts off the conditions of a different model. But, one may ask, what about Sundays? Was Rutherford perhaps reserving those days for the un-modelled mystery of both qualities happening simultaneously? Was he, with his canny Scots background, careful not to exclude God? Was he simply taking days off for necessary meditation and reflection on the broader implications of his problems? Or, like a good teacher, was he allowing us to see for

---

FIGURE 6-3   **Interference of light explained by the wave theory**

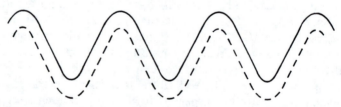

Two waves 'in phase' and therefore reinforcing each other.

Two waves 'out of phase' cancel each other out.

---

ourselves that the dual nature of electron behaviour depends on how we look at it. If we set up experiments designed to detect particles we will see electrons as particles — we will be working in a Newtonian world. But if we move to the Einsteinian world and use equipment to detect waves, we will be rewarded with the conclusion that electrons show wave properties. As with more elementary observations, we see what we want to see; as long as we confine ourselves to one model or world we remain blind to the views available from another. It is therefore possible to make our model into a cage; we may mistake it for the reality it was designed to clarify.

The danger in confusing the model with reality

The temptation to see only what we want to see is greater in more complex and less exact sciences like psychology. A model, however crude, may be helpful in using abstract ideas but it can lead to errors if used uncritically as a hard fact, and not as a useful fiction. Just as Aristotle's successors ignored his advice not to regard the *psyche* as a physical part of the body, so many modern educationists find it hard to remember that intelligence is not an entity that can be measured as precisely as the size of one's head.

At one time the intelligence quotient (IQ) seemed to be a more reliable guide for the assessment of mental agility; however the basis of quantifiable data, the aura of scientific respectability, the phrase itself, all give an illusion of solidity to what is essentially a relatively flimsy concept. Alfred Binet, who first attempted to measure intelligence in order to identify those children who might need special educational help, foresaw some dangers. He wrote: 'For the sake of simplicity of statement, we will speak of a child of 8 years having the intelligence of a child of 7 or 9 years; but these expressions, if accepted arbitrarily, may give place to illusions.' In many instances his warning has gone unheeded; the IQ (mental age divided by actual age) — a concept associated with Binet but one which he did not actually invent — has often been derived from tests which depend as much on information and from experience as on innate intelligence.

There is little doubt about the variation of intelligence among human beings; doubtless intelligence is due in part to genetic factors but it may be influenced by early training and by a stimulating environment. It can reveal itself in a variety of ways, for example in the solution of abstract problems or in the unravelling of more practical technological puzzles; and although it combines successfully with the amassing of knowledge in traditional education, it often works most efficiently when uncluttered by what is seen, in retro-spect, as irrelevant information. It is still a hazy and partly mysterious concept which, unfortunately, seems to have become crystallized into something assumed to be fully understood.

IQ tests have therefore been used to justify racism and to direct people to occupations for which they are not suited. They have been permitted to decide the type of education, either predominantly intellectual or practical, which eleven-year-old children should follow. Our present comprehensive secondary education may be far from perfect but it certainly does not, at the moment, embody the false and often self-fulfilling belief that we can determine a child's educational potential from a very early age. In his book, *The Mismeasure of Man*, Professor Stephen Jay Gould writes: 'We pass through this world but once. Few tragedies can be more extensive than the stunting of life, few injustices deeper than the denial of an opportunity to strive or even to hope, by a limit imposed from without but falsely identified as lying within.'

The value of models in the progress of science

In 1962, Thomas Kuhn offered an explanation of the progress of science in terms of the periodic creation of models, or *paradigms* as he named them. A paradigm is a simplified, imaginary 'world' created by scientists in order to explain and explore the real world. Kuhn's book, *The Structure of Scientific Revolutions*, was very influential, even fashionable; in particular it encouraged some readers to try to find yet more parallels between the obviously successful physical sciences and the social and political sciences, economics and even history. This search is to be admired and encouraged; there is mutual benefit in the comparison of the scientific method developed from the more exact sciences with modes of thought applicable to less exact sciences.

But one of Kuhn's lessons is often ignored. Within the models or paradigms, argument and experiment may precisely match each other, yet they may resemble only superficially the events of the real world; there is then a tendency to misinterpret or overlook real events in order to make the real world match the model. Thus politicians may construct for themselves paradigms in which argu-ments about theories of economics, or policies shaped by past events in history, are convincing and impeccably reasonable; but, because these created worlds are not the real world, we should not be surprised that the argument and policies, in confrontation with the harsh facts of life, are eventually shown to be wrong. Perhaps we ought not to be surprised that the politicians, unlike ideal scientists, so often remain faithful to outworn paradigms; the belief dies hard that what has worked well in the past will continue to do so even if the circumstances of the problem have completely changed.

Kuhn himself would not be surprised by such intransigence. He believes that most scientists do not actually expose dubious theories for criticism by other scientists, that they accept the current paradigm, and work within it to support it. This is why, he claims, a paradigm lasts so long and why revolutions in science are so rare. Moreover, he asserts that this loyalty to the paradigm is necessary for the existence of science because it leads to corporate effort instead of individual wrangling about objectives; in doing so, he directly challenges Popper—'it is precisely the abandonment of critical discourse that marks the transition to science.'

It may be that Kuhn, perhaps even with his tongue in his cheek, is being deliberately down-to-earth here. The Popperian ideal of setting up one's cherished theory as a target may seem too lofty for the average scientist who, like any other human being, feels an unconscious pull towards certainty and familiarity; the rebel has a more uncomfortable time than the conformist. It may also be that Kuhn's interpretation of the uncertain progress of science through the ages, taking human weakness into account, is basically sound and not at all cynical. However, there is little doubt that Popper's recipe for advancement is, in retrospect, correct; models will, sooner or later, collapse when they no longer match the real world. The Copernican model of the universe did not replace the Ptolemaic overnight; learned men of the time fought to retain the old model and Copernicus himself kept quiet about the new; but the newer model was finally established and, in its turn, superseded, even if we still cling to its remnants in our small corner of the universe.

Popper himself, on being told that scientists do not always behave in the ideal manner he describes, is reported to have said: 'Well, they should.' With his precepts in mind we can set off into the fog, confident that we shall find the right road; but if at times we prefer to linger with others at a convenient resting place and subsequently move on together, we are simply being human, if less adventurous.

The model as a substitute for reality

Those who do set out on their own are increasingly beset by doubts. *Is* there a single path to truth? Is not one path merely a matter of choice? Do we not simply end up at a different part of the same truth, depending on what path we first selected? Does the path chosen merge with other paths? May it not even end up where it started? Perhaps the truth is so complicated that we will ultimately see only what we want to see or what educational and other influences have conditioned us to see. Perhaps the model that we have created is all that we can hope to understand.

This is a common predicament and writers of all ages have recorded it. We have already met Walter Mitty but he was preceded, some 400 years ago, by Don Quixote who tilted at windmills, imagining that they were giants. Both men have created dream worlds so that they can live in them, safe from the cold winds of reality. Don Quixote deliberately avoids exposing his illusions to any test that might admit these cold winds. But Walter Mitty has one foot in the real world; he adapts his dreams to suit the real occasion and therefore makes effective use of them as a protection against the winds. Carl Gustav Jung would approve!

CHAPTER SEVEN

Effects

Until about 1650 one gets an impression of the wholeness of the worlds of thought and nature in English literature. From the mid-century the gulf, which is the gulf between the arts and sciences, becomes increasingly obvious. For a variety of reasons ... English style was to grow simpler, less metaphorical and less allusive, while the interest of writers was directed increasingly to good sense, rather than involved feelings.
— *J. F. West*

My first rule was to accept nothing as true which I did not clearly recognise to be so; to accept nothing more than what was presented to my mind so clearly and distinctly that I would have no occasion to doubt it. The second rule was to divide each problem or difficulty into as many parts as possible. The third rule was to commence my reflections with the simplest and easiest to understand, and rise thence, little by little, to knowledge of the most complex. The fourth rule was to make enumerations so complete, and reviews so general, that I should be certain to have omitted nothing.
— *René Descartes (his method for attacking philosophical problems)*

The steam engine helped to shape the modern world at least as much as Napoleon and Adam Smith.
— *Sir Charles Snow*

Marxist philosophy holds that the most important problem does not lie in understanding the laws of the objective world and thus being able to explain it, but in applying the knowledge of these laws actively to change the world.
— *Mao Tse-tung*

Copernicus showed that we live on a peripheral hunk of rock, but we could still believe that God put us there by fiat. Darwin proved that we had evolved naturally, but we still had our rational minds. Freud denied our rationality but we could still view our mental power as unique. Now we must admit that a board of silicon chips might surpass all the cognitive power in our heads.
— *Stephen Jay Gould*

My atheism, like that of Spinoza, is true piety towards the universe and denies only gods fashioned by men in their own image to be servants of their human interests.
— *George Santayana*

When a man is freed of religion, he has a better chance to live a normal and wholesome life.
— *Sigmund Freud*

Science without religion is lame, religion without science is blind.
— *Albert Einstein*

Questions . . .

In what ways has science contributed to women's liberation?

We have made tools like the wheel, the lever, and the computer. To what extent is it true to say that tools continue to shape us?

Has the increased use of calculators helped or hindered us in the understanding of mathematics?

What has the history of science to offer a student of English?

Can a scientist be a Christian?

'The novel *Frankenstein* is a parable about science and technology.' How?

Why, at present, is there such an interest in the occult?

Science shapes human development

If you put an iron (or steel) nail into a solution of copper sulphate the nail will soon become coated with copper. But if you put a piece of copper into a solution of iron sulphate nothing happens. The chemist infers that iron is more 'active' than copper and that therefore, in forming compounds more easily, it will replace the copper in copper sulphate.

The turbulent centuries in our early history known as the Bronze and Iron Ages were shaped by this simple difference in chemical properties. The legends of ancient Crete, the sagas of the Cleopatras, all began from the relatively easy extraction of copper from its compounds and the discovery that bronze, a blend of copper and tin, is harder, more durable, and more versatile than copper itself. Iron was harder to isolate and was initially very crude. But it was more plentiful and more widespread, and its development meant the collapse of the 'monopoly' of copper-based civilizations.

As we have seen in the introduction, science and history have interacted from the earliest times. The invention and uses of tools and weapons demanded new skills from their users. By the principle of the survival of the fittest, those who could use these devices most effectively grew in number compared with those who could not. And the process continues. This so-called scientific age in which we live is not simply the result of our dependence on technological gadgets; our whole way of life and thought has been shaped and directed by the scientific framework into which we have been born. Average citizens of today are not only more knowledgeable than our counterparts in the Middle Ages; we are also more intelligent. How this increased intelligence is used is, of course, another matter.

This scientific effect has its negative side. As an apparently trivial example, consider the effect of pocket calculators on school-children. Such machines have removed the drudgery from calculations but, in many cases, they have made simple arithmetical processes more mysterious and caused many children to shun the type of mental arithmetic which is both beneficial as exercise and possibly quicker than the calculator. It is interesting that many adults are becoming aware of the physical results of over-dependence on the motor car but they are not so concerned with the mental flabbiness arising from over-dependence on the calculator.

On a larger scale, computerized machinery is designed by the intelligent few to replace the mental and manual skills of the majority. Robots can be designed to build and maintain cars but robots, like the pocket calculator, have no brains. If one's job is merely the supervision of robots there is a real danger that the type of skill which has contributed to the development of human intelligence will, for many people, be lost. As industry relies increasingly on automation the problem will be heightened by the increase in leisure time. This is why there is a growing interest in the idea of education for leisure, for living instead of only making a living; the more valuable schemes for such education will almost certainly favour the stimulation of practical, creative, and critical skills.

The Industrial Revolution puts science 'on the map'

The changes in the Western world in the last three centuries are more remarkabe than those in earlier epochs only because they have been more rapid. Before the dawn of the modern science the universe around us and the world in particular were observed, discussed, and puzzled over; but apart from some local interference with nature there was little thought of meddling with our environment. Most people were content 'to be'; the urge nowadays is 'to do.'

This change did not take place overnight, and it did not happen only because of the work of Copernicus, Kepler, Galileo, or even Newton. Indeed, after Newton had assembled the huge astronomical jigsaw puzzle started by his predecessors there was a distinct pause in the study of astronomy, the centre of scientific activity at the time. Newton had apparently removed all the mystery from the universe and there seemed little more to be done. But gradually the scientific method which had proved so successful in dispelling astronomical mysteries was applied, particularly through the medium of the Royal Society, to more mundane problems of industry. The relationship between pure science and engineering, between ideas and practice, had existed only accidentally and spasmodically in earlier times; now that it was more frequently seen to produce desirable social results it was deliberately developed.

As a consequence of the growing demands of industry, James Watt's steam engine appeared at the beginning of the nineteenth century. In its early form it had many shortcomings but it was efficient enough to delight its industrial sponsors and to encourage them to demand scientifically designed improvements. The focus of scientific research thus shifted to the study of energy. Electricity was developed, the potential of coal and coal-gas was explored, the internal combustion engine was invented. Buildings, roads, and cities spread widely; public transport and communication were transformed. The surface of a large part of the civilized world was radically changed largely because of this increasing inter-dependence of science, technology, and industry; to paraphrase C. P. Snow's statement, the steam engine helped to shape the modern world at least as much as military leaders, politicians, and economists.

But these sweeping changes also had a profound effect on the outlook of the average family. New modes of employment meant new living standards; the new science which hitherto had begun to change the mental atmosphere of a few academics now began to disturb the way of life and of thought of ordinary people. Newtonian ideas may have meant little to the average man or woman but if they were the root cause of the success of the new industries they were clearly to be respected and encouraged.

Reasons for the growth of chemistry

New sciences appeared. Soon chemistry was literally to make life more colourful by the invention of new dyes, and to provide a new stimulus to the already flourishing textile industry. The growing scientific confidence made it possible to replace the mystical influence of the alchemist by a framework of quantitative chemical theory; vague alchemical principles gave way to firm laws such as the Law of Conservation of Matter which indicated that matter could not be created or destroyed, but merely moved from one combination to another. The perceptive scientist might have detected a warning note here; the amount of iron in the world, for example, is limited and we could not go on using it without, one day, facing a shortage. But that day was a long way off and, in any case, the law itself was a reminder that discarded iron could be used again, or, as we would now describe it, recycled.

For a long time it was assumed that organic chemistry, the chemistry of living things, depended upon a mysterious spark of life and was therefore beyond human investigation. But in 1828 Wohler took inorganic materials and synthesized a substance which had previously been extracted only from organic matter. The chemistry of living organisms, although more complex, was revealed as essentially the same as that of inorganic material—a fact that modern writers on gardening, who deplore the feeding of the soil with 'chemicals' instead of honest manure, could ponder.

Effects of the new chemistry on other sciences

The subsequent development of biochemistry had incalculable effects both on geology and medicine. Cutting through large sections of hillsides for road and railway construction had exposed many valuable geological phenomena, and the new chemistry opened the way to deeper study of fossils of extinct species and to a new view of the age of the Earth. The effect on medicine, the ability to examine chemical processes in the body, was not so immediate; doubts persisted that science could not cope with matters of life and death. Nevertheless, as early as the 1840s, chemistry was beginning to change the ways of medicine with the introduction of anaesthetics such as nitrous oxide ('laughing gas'). Changes were slow because the simple methodology initiated by Hippocrates was still very effective; the new scientific atmosphere simply justified and refined existing techniques.

It was a combination of careful observation and accurate experiment, rather than complex theorizing, which led Edward Jenner (1749–1823) to discover the benefits of vaccination. In the spreading slum conditions brought about by the Industrial Revolution it became obvious that there was a connection between disease and bad sanitation; even without knowing the precise nature of this connection, doctors could take simple precautionary measures to control the spread of disease. The link was made clear when Louis Pasteur (1822−1895) established his germ theory. As in the relationship between smoking and cancer, a connection seemed highly probable if not certain; Pasteur confirmed it with his discovery of germs which, although invisible and intangible like the vapours and evil spirits of ancient times, can be shown by simple experiment to have real existence.

Continued unscientific attitude to mental health

Just as people now go to the zoo to see the animals, it was fashionable, as recently as the early eighteenth century, to visit Bedlam, the hospital of St. Mary of Bethlehem in London, to watch the insane inmates. It was the view of the general public, as well as of many members of the medical profession, that these unfortunates were beyond human help, that they were possessed by evil spirits or devils. A more sympathetic approach to the problems of the mentally ill was already established by the beginning of the nineteenth century but it was not until Sigmund Freud, early in this century, began his monumental work on the function of the unconscious mind that these problems were properly appreciated.

Freud reacted to the lingering popular belief that madness had supernatural origins by a scientific study of abnormal mental behaviour. He was able to show that irrational lapses of which we are all capable may be due to suppression of those primitive desires which, if we wish to remain civilized and on good terms with other people, we must try to contain. He suggested that the retention of these desires in our unconscious minds was revealed in dreams (when the conscious suppression is relaxed) or even in occasional slips of the tongue when a hidden truth bypasses the barrier of civilized conversation. Sometimes the suppression fails and the result may be an explosion of violent behaviour; if it succeeds completely the pressure of pent-up emotion may produce varying degrees of mental illness.

Some of Freud's critics felt that his methods were too scientific, too restricted to the coldly rational side of human experience. Jung's work sought to satisfy the desire for fantasy in our lives. Other critics believed that Freud was not scientific enough, that he had merely substituted one set of myths for another; they pointed to the success of Ivan Pavlov (1849−1936) who had successfully demonstrated that much animal behaviour is conditioned, simply by practical experience, that we acquire new skills, like driving a car, by repetitive practice until we can perform them 'without thinking.' As a result of this scientific view of psychology the 'behaviourist school' was created; it aimed to explain human behaviour in terms of the responses of the human body to outside stimuli and of the consequent chemical changes within the body.

Although the process of demystification has continued, the hunger for fantasy which concerned Jung is not easily satisfied and exlusively scientific theories about the functioning of the human mind certainly do not convince everyone. It is disturbing to note that, in the last few decades, there has been a marked popular regression to more highly coloured views of mental illness with a revival of the practice of exorcism to expel devils from the insane mind.

Growth of popular confidence in science

During the eighteenth century the image of science as the great public benefactor shone more and more brightly. Progress was a new and intoxicating idea; the ancient world had been pessimistic about human destiny and for centuries the Christian Church had insisted that we aim in vain for perfection. Now the average person could look forward to a healthier, more prosperous future than the wildest dreams of the peasant of earlier centuries.

Early in the scientific revolution John Donne (1572–1631) had written:

> And new Philosophy calls all in doubt,
> The Element of Fire is quite put out;
> The Sun is lost, and th' Earth, and no man's wit
> Can well direct him where to look for it.

But after Newton had revealed a universal order, Alexander Pope (1688–1744) wrote:

> Nature and Nature's laws lay hid in night;
> God said "Let Newton be" and all was light.

In our own time, J. B. Priestley has commented on Pope's couplet thus:

> Notice the air of confidence and cheerful pride, the suggestion that at last all was known, their hint that God can now retire. . . . Darkness, with all that was unknown, mysterious, superhuman, magical, fateful, has vanished. Reason, the enquiring and experimenting mind, brings everything into the light. So, very soon, all the enlightened, if they allowed God still to exist, regarded him as a remote first cause, who had put together and then set in motion the vast but smoothly running well-oiled machine of the

universe. God did not intervene in human affairs; worship and prayer were wasted efforts; men should study nature and use their reason ... It would be difficult to find two other lines of verse that would tell us more about the eighteenth century than these two.

Evolution and religion

And, of course, there was much more to come. Not only were the landscape of the civilized world and the way of life of most of its inhabitants completely transformed in the nineteenth century; the worlds of thought and of human aspiration were radically redirected; the process of demystification, the gradual shedding of veils of superstition that had impeded for so long the path of scientific progress seemed to be almost complete. The work of Charles Darwin appeared to be the final stage of the process; it was said that 'everything is evolving and the direction of evolution is, by definition, good.'

When Darwin's theories, on *The Origin of Species*, were published in 1859 the idea of evolution was not new. Lamarck had recently revived an old idea, that characteristics such as strength or mental power could be handed down from parent to child. Darwin's contribution, backed up by an impressive range of observations, showed that progress from less able to more efficient forms of life was due to chance variations in a species; these variations ensured the survival only of those best equipped to cope with changing circumstances. In the prevailing scientific climate his ideas seemed clear and convincing, especially after the work of Mendel (published in 1865 and 1869) on the genetic mechanism of inheritance was seen to support them. But in religious circles, where the effects of the new cosmology were still felt, the ideas were not so welcome; Lamarck's views were in accordance with the Christian urge towards self-improvement but Darwin's seemed to point to a God who was either less than omnipotent or a gambler.

If we think of religion partly as an attempt to explain natural mysteries and partly as a guide for human behaviour, it is the first part which is most immediately altered by science. When, like children, we saw ourselves at the centre of the universe we could imagine some sort of heavenly father far above us. But this image was destroyed by Copernicus. The discarded model had required a supernatural force to keep it going but the Copernican model, refined by Newton, needed no such force — once the process had started. Disturbing questions were raised; if humans are the chief actors in God's drama, why is the stage so immense and empty and why are we given such a tiny corner of it? And, with the arrival of ideas about evolution, if God has a master plan why this element of chance which Darwin has introduced? Or if it is not chance, why is the plan so wasteful of many species?

Science and religion continue to diverge

The gulf between science and religion, first obvious after the discoveries of Copernicus and Galileo, now widened. The dilemma of the thinking individual, perhaps wanting to believe in a creator but trying to keep a scientifically open mind, became more acute. In earlier times the mental split was not so worrying. Newton was a devout Christian for all his life: it is ironic that, although the implications of his discoveries have since led many away from religion, Newton himself seemed unaffected and indeed, was prouder of work on alchemy and mysticism which we now regard as worthless. Perhaps, like many of today's believers, he assumed that science can never remove fundamental mysteries. But great mysteries of the past have been explained and there is no reason to suppose that present mysteries will not eventually disappear in the clarifying light of science. The true scientist will have this attitude. But any scientists who accept that some mysteries are impossible to solve will either stop searching for truth or will unconsciously select only the evidence that matches their preconceived ideas; they will therefore have stopped being scientists. Any attempt to form an alliance between science and the supernatural is doomed to failure because, as Popper has demonstrated, beliefs about the existence of God, however valuable to an individual in search of spiritual solace, are outside the range of science.

Psychology as a substitute for religion?

Just as the new astronomy and biology provided acceptable rational explanations for physical mysteries, it seemed for a time that psychology would be a more appropriate modern guide to spiritual problems than the wisdom of Christ, of Buddha, or of the myth-makers of Ancient Greece. Certainly no science has had more effect on popular culture than psychology; it is impossible to consider a modern novel or play without reference to the language, at least, of pioneers of psychology like Freud or Jung.

Up to a point the substitution was not only acceptable but positively illuminating if applied to faded religious clichés. 'The Kingdom of Heaven is within you' could be an incentive to attain individual peace of mind or to aim at the creation of an ideal community; 'he who hath seen me hath seen the Father' hinted that there is something of God in every man and that it could be persuaded to grow towards the perfection that was Christ; 'God is love' suggested that the very idea of God was a personification of the compassion and respect for others, essential for the ideal earthly paradise towards which we should all strive. All these, and other basic truths formerly expressed poetically, could be examined in a fresh light and given new shades of meaning in practical terms.

Jung, however, insisted that psychology as a science could not completely replace religion; some of the old mythology, viewed afresh in the light of modern developments, had to be retained. He called himself a Protestant in the sense that he criticized the traditional teachings of particular churches; but, for anyone who felt the need of a church, he recommended the Roman Catholic church for its ritual and symbolism. He could not define God but he claimed that he had convinced himself that the pattern of God exists in every human being, providing the energy for self-improvement and liberation. He believed that the question of good and evil had nothing to do with remote metaphysics; 'it is only a concern of psychology.'

Jung's brand of psychology contains the idea that aggressive instincts are predominantly masculine while more gentle, compassionate behaviour is feminine. But each of us, he claims, contains both masculine and feminine qualities; too much of one would produce a violent, murderous personality while too much of the other might lead to apathy in the face of evil. Human unhappiness, on both personal and world levels, is caused by the unnatural separation in our daily lives of the two qualities. The idea recalls the Yin-Yang concept and the 'humours' of the alchemists; Jung acknowledges his debt to these symbols.

It is the presence of this idea in Roman Catholicism which explains Jung's approval of a recent controversial proclamation by the Roman Catholic Church. Just as each of us is born biologically from woman, so Jung (echoing the Christian 'ye must be born again') believed that we can have psychological rebirth through the feminine, or non-aggressive, parts of our nature; in other words, the feminine characterstics are the means by which we can bring together the warring elements in our personalities. One proclamation by the Roman Catholic authorities concerned the bodily assumption of the Virgin Mary into Heaven. Many rationalist critics saw this as a step backwards into superstition, but Jung saw it as a recipe in living Christian symbolism embracing both human and supernatural ideas, for spiritual or psychological wholeness.

Unfortunately, Jung's rationalist critics are over-literal in their interpretation of much symbolism. They have fallen into the same trap as those disciples of Christ or the Buddha, of Aristotle or even of Newton, who crystallized valuable but nebulous advice into inflexible rules, who translated poetic suggestions for our common benefit into fixed guidelines. Psychology has increasing potential to enhance the well-being of us all; but misguided attempts to see it as an exact science may, instead, make of it another narrow religion which, if it does not provide instant comfort, may well be rejected.

How science has affected literature

Science affects the way we think, and the more clearly we think the more clearly we write. As the influence of the new science of the sixteenth century spread, so those who wrote about it gradually dropped the fashionable, highly decorative style of medieval writers in favour of clear, unambiguous prose. Words had often been used — not always deliberately — to conceal truth behind a complex verbal pattern; now writers began to aim at clarity of communication rather than stylishness for its own sake. Galileo's description of what he saw with his telescope avoids all poetic and pseudopoetic language and records his observations concisely and without fuss. The effect of this on popular understanding is obvious.

Francis Bacon was among the first to see in scientific method a guide in the search for truth; it is not surprising that he is the author of the statement: 'reading maketh a full man, conference a ready man and writing an exact man.' Even a glance at the selections from his writings in a dictionary of quotations reveals Bacon as the clearest of communicators. He wished to free humans from the cramping influence of authority and to convince us of the power of our own searching minds. He was aware of the trap of common sense — 'the mind resembles those uneven mirrors which impart their own properties to different objects' — but he was also conscious of the dangers in even the simplest language — 'the idols imposed upon the understanding by words are of two kinds. They are either the names of things which have no existence (for example 'fortune' and 'element of fire') or they are the names of actual objects but confused, badly defined, and hastily and irregularly abstracted from things.' Words mean only what we want them to mean; confusion in language can lead only to distortion of the image of truth.

The changes in views of the universe and of the human race's position in it were increasingly discussed or referred to in literature; thus the new ideas became widespread. Shakespeare's plays show a fascinating blend of the older way of thought with the new. On the one hand, we read in *The Merchant of Venice*:

Look how the floor of heaven
Is thick inlaid with patines of bright gold;
There's not the smallest orb which thou beholdest
But in his motion like an angel sings.

whereas in *Julius Caesar* there is the famous denial of the power of astrology:

The fault, dear Brutus, is not in our stars
But in ourselves that we are underlings.

Elsewhere in *Julius Caesar* there is a wealth of superstition which is more of Shakespeare's time than of Caesar's; it was at this time — a time not unlike our own when we are trying to come to terms with another new view of the universe — that humankind was torn between loyalty to old beliefs and the attraction of the new.

Even the tools of the new science opened up fresh worlds of imagination. In *Science and the Imagination*, Marjorie Nicolson points out that Shakespeare lived in a world of time whereas Milton inhabited a universe of space. The 'wooden O' of Shakespeare's Globe Theatre is the actor's universe with the actor at the centre; its space is so limited that it has little significance for the writer. Not so with the universe which Milton evokes in *Paradise Lost* — a vast, limitless emptiness. Milton's vision had been broadened by acquaintance with the new cosmology; he had reputedly visited Galileo during his Italian journey and had used a telescope to see deeply into space. The experience stimulated his imagination but it disturbed his religious views; in his subsequent writings he referred to the possibility of an Infinite Deity, a concept which conflicted with his earlier beliefs.

The first flush of enthusiasm for the early successes of science was not universal. In *Gulliver's Travels* (1726) Swift poked fun at those who merely replaced old superstitions with new. He feared that the supporters of science might uncritically accept its teachings in the same way that they formerly believed in magic. He had detected the same danger that Aristotle had foreseen at the time of his death, that scientific discoveries would be regarded as truth, and that the more reliable scientific way of thought would be neglected. But his warnings were generally unheeded as the effects of science were made more widespread during the Industrial Revolution. Freedom from superstition and from extremes of poverty seemed more attainable but, by the middle of the nineteenth century, reaction to the advancement of science had sharpened. Mary Shelley's *Frankenstein*, a scientist, created a monster which he could not control and which eventually destroyed him; readers saw in the novel a parable about the godlessness of a science which was already sweeping away cherished ways of life with old beliefs.

Today, even in its many coarsened film versions, the story has much to tell us, not only about dissilusionment with science but about hunger for a more certain truth.

It was this hunger that prompted William Blake to reject science and John Keats to protest against its 'deadening hand.' But there were writers who accepted the inevitability of new ways of thought and of social change, not passively but with a positive welcome for fresh challenges. William Wordsworth (1770–1850) had read mathematics at Cambridge and greatly respected Newton; he subsequently wove the scientific outlook into the pattern of his poetry and his philosophy of life. 'If every event in the world and even in the mind of man can ultimately be explained by natural laws it seems that man himself is a fleeting consciousness imprisoned in the body and doomed to extinction when the body dissolves.' But instead of protesting against it, or simply ignoring it, Wordsworth found the challenge invigorating, and the new clarity of vision a source of joy.

Changes in social and political thought

Throughout the Dark Ages people had been encouraged to believe in a natural order of things, both in the cosmos and in society. Sun, moon, and planets moved in fixed paths around the Earth; the Earth itself was the natural repository for earthy materials and the outermost sphere in the universe was the natural place for fire; that was why rocks fell and flames leaped upwards. It must be the same in society; a peasant's true home was his hovel and every prince had his palace and if, as so many myths and fairytales remind us, anything went wrong with this scheme of things, both prince and peasant would eventually find their true places.

With the development of science it was a matter of time before people began to look at their positions in society with more critical eyes. Criticism is at the very heart of the process of thought that we call science; the true scientist does not jealously protect an idea from criticism but welcomes it as an aid to improvement. In this context, criticism is not a sour process of fault-finding; faults *are* found but with the purpose of eliminating them. So, if the scientific ideas, first communicated by Bacon in England and Descartes in France, successfully encouraged scientists to find radical new ways of looking at the universe, could not similar ideas bring about miracles of change in society?

Thomas Hobbes (1588–1679) felt that the new ideas could be applied to mental, spiritual, and political problems. In *Leviathan* he tried to show that scientific laws could explain the behaviour of human beings in society. Perhaps he was too optimistic about accuracy in prediction in such circumstances, but he was pessimistic enough to suggest that humans would need control from some authority if they were not to destroy one another.

John Locke (1632–1704) had been greatly influenced by Newton and he, too, believed that science could make improvements in the human condition, although he was less pessimistic than Hobbes about mankind's fate; in his *Essay Concerning Human Understanding* he suggested that man should eventually be able to control himself without outside authority. He compared a child's mind with a blank piece of paper on which experience writes; every person, in his view, creates their own world and must therefore solve their own unique problems with fresh ideas, not with outworn solutions of the past. In Locke's writings we see the seeds of modern psychology together with hints of the twentieth century philosophy of existentialism.

Such views, critical of the *status quo* in society, first flourished in England and contributed to its Civil War; a modern historian has pointed out that the Cavalier party contained all the notable followers of Ptolemy and the Roundheads all the Copernicans. This is not to say that the Puritan mind had been directly trained by science but, nevertheless, its critical, probing way of thought was scientific. Many Puritans turned to science because they had lost faith in old beliefs, both religious and political, and they were equally cautious about accepting new ideas which had yet to be tested.

The social changes which they caused were consequently slow to take place, but long-lasting. It was not so in France; there the ruling aristocracy unsuccessfully tried to ignore or suppress criticism and, when the changes did occur, they were more explosive, more bloody, and ultimately more unstable.

Karl Marx (1818–1883)

Political changes stemming directly or indirectly from science continued to take place. The various Marxist movements of today started with a man who, like so many other eighteenth and nineteenth century thinkers, believed that humanity could make progress towards perfection. Karl Marx's most influential ideas had already appeared when Darwin's *Origin of Species* was published; but it is virtually certain that the same ideas about evolution motivated both.

In fact, Marx wanted to dedicate the second volume of *Das Kapital* to Darwin, an honour which Darwin, in view of his professed ignorance of economic science, declined. As Isaiah Berlin, Marx's biographer, puts it: 'he had a greater intellectual admiration (for

Darwin) than for any other of his contemporaries, regarding him as having done for the morphology of the natural sciences what he himself was striving to do for human history.' Marx wanted his theories to parallel proved scientific theories; in *Das Kapital* he claims to have discovered 'the Natural Laws of capitalist production' and that it is his aim to 'lay bare the Economic Law of Motion of Modern Society' so that such laws will work 'with iron necessity towards inevitable results.'

Marx may seem a shade dogmatic compared with the scientist's cautious approach to problems; but he did, with limited success, test some of his theories in the field of revolutionary politics. But many predictions from them were found to be inaccurate and some of Marx's disciples reacted by reformulating the theories. According to Karl Popper in *The Open Society and Its Enemies*, their aim was not to improve the accordance of theory and evidence but to disguise the inconsistencies of the theories and to make further falsification impossible. Popper saw that the acceptance of one of these theories had 'the effect of an intellectual conversion or revelation, opening your eyes to a new truth hidden from those not yet initiated. Once your eyes were thus opened you saw confirming instances everywhere; the world was full of *verifications* of the theory.'

In other words, what started out as at least partly scientific has now become, because of this protection from criticism, this immunity to falsification, a non-science. It therefore gives rise to illusions of certainty which have no place in any science but which have similarities to religious beliefs. Commenting on the views of the economist Milton Friedman, Eric Roll writes: 'this complete absence of philosophic doubt, this consciousness of superior knowledge through having received the revelation, are the hallmarks of doctrines (Marxism is another such) which partake of the nature of religion.' Many Marxists are therefore doubly wrong; not only is Marxism at best a partial science but *any* science progresses *because* of doubt towards a knowledge which can never be clearly foreseen. Science, as Popper describes it, can never magically realize the Utopian dream of 'maximizing happiness' but, if we are willing, it can be steered in apparently the opposite direction in an attempt to 'minimize avoidable suffering.' Such a course of action would both highlight immediate problems and more quickly and practically lead to their removal.

Bishop Berkeley's distrust of science

In the next section we shall remind ourselves that the generally optimistic view of science which prevailed till the beginning of the twentieth century was bound to create a reaction of doubt and distrust. We may reflect that science, like a surgical instrument, cannot be blamed if someone uses it for evil purposes; but we must remind ourselves that, even while it is distrusted, science continues to shape the ways in which we think and behave.

Before we do, let us consider the disturbing views of one eighteenth century philosopher who distrusted the value of scientific thought. George Berkeley (1685–1753), philosopher, man of the Church, and trenchant critic of the materialism of Newtonian science, argued that, since all the essentially unreliable evidence for scientific theories must come to us through our senses, we have no convincing proof that anything at all exists outside our minds. Even if two people agree about the colour and hardness of a cricket ball, it does not follow that there is any objective truth in the statement, 'the cricket ball is red'; and there is no way of showing that the hardness is any proof of the ball's solidity or even of its existence. What appears to be red to one viewer might appear blue to the other and, because each has always associated the word 'red' with what he or she sees as red, neither will ever know that individual experiences are different. Like colour, the feeling of hardness is interpreted by the brain and is equally subjective. Samuel Johnson, author, lexicographer, and apostle of common sense, was told of these ideas; it would be impossible, his informant said, to refute the notion that stone did not exist. Johnson promptly kicked away the stone and retorted: 'Sir, I refute it thus.' But unfortunately the idea cannot be removed as easily as the stone.

One comment on Berkeley's ideas was:

> *There once was a man who said "God*
> *Must find it exceedingly odd*
> *If he finds that this tree*
> *Continues to be*
> *When there's no one about in the quad."*

To which there is a reply:

> *Dear Sir: Your astonishment's odd.*
> *I am always about in the quad;*
> *And that's why this tree*
> *Continues to be,*
> *Since observed by Yours faithfully, God*

Clearly, Berkeley's ideas gave much consolation to the Church and they tended to be dismissed as hair-splitting by science. But science cannot afford to ignore such views. In a world in which a growing number of scientific and technological achievements pointed to the triumph of Newtonian science it was easy to dismiss the views as

useless fantasy; but they were a timely reminder that things are
never necessarily what they seem. We can now see that Berkeley's
ideas have, directly or indirectly, led to scientific concepts which
are even stranger; the wonderland of modern physics with
its empty atoms, warped time scales, and multiple co-existent
universes — each unaware of the existence of any others — seems
just as crazy as anything Berkeley imagined. On a more mundane
level we now accept the idea of psychosomatic illness, by which
the very thought of illness can produce physical symptoms; and we
have begun to understand how increased mental stress can produce a
variety of bodily complaints. There is more 'reality' in ideas like
Berkeley's than was once believed by scientific thinkers and the
true scientist considers them very carefully to find what they may
have to offer.

Berkeley's ideas may have provided some consolation for
theologians but, by the nineteenth century, they could only have
increased the bewilderment of formerly religious folk, now aware
of the inadequacies of traditional beliefs from which they used to
derive comfort. They might continue to pay lip-service to religious
practice 'just in case ...' but they had decided that science had
more immediate benefits to offer. Despite biblical assurances of a
lifespan of threescore years and ten, average citizens of the eighteenth century died at the age of 48; as a result of the tentative but
confident progress of nineteenth century medicine, their counterparts could expect to live to 67. There was, as yet, little reason to
doubt science as the fount of all wisdom, the dispeller of mystery
and superstition.

Even in the world of science itself the mood of confidence
prevailed. True, there were a few loose ends to be tied up. The new
wealth of energy was not unlimited — the Law of Conservation of
Energy was a reminder that all known sources merely stored finite
amounts from the sun — but this did not seem to be any more
significant than that the amount of water in the sea was limited.
There was the problem of the sun itself; where did it get its
apparently infinite energy? And there were some new and strange
phenomena; a chemical element, helium, was discovered by analysis
of the sun's rays before it was isolated on Earth; there was the odd
behaviour of recently discovered forms of radiation like X-rays and
cathode rays. But such eccentricities were generally pushed aside
by the triumphant progress of mainstream science; as Kuhn would
describe it, the aim of the average scientist was to consolidate the
impressive structure for which Newton had provided the blueprint,
and to assume that a place would eventually be found for any
strange new discoveries.

If now, looking back on the subtle changes of thought at the

CHAPTER EIGHT

Doubts

Philosophy calls all in doubt.
— *John Donne*

True science teaches, above all, to doubt and be ignorant.
— *de Unamuno*

Science should leave off making pronouncements; the river of knowledge has too often turned back on itself.
— *Sir James Jeans*

If anything can go wrong, it will.
Corollary 1: Even if nothing can possibly go wrong, it will anyway.
Corollary 2: Whatever goes wrong, there is always somebody who knew it would.
— *Law attributed to Murphy, or Finagle, or Sod.*

As far as the propositions of mathematics refer to reality, they are not certain . . . and as far as they are certain, they do not refer to reality.
— *Albert Einstein*

Those who are not shocked when they first come across quantum theory cannot possibly have understood it.
— *Niels Bohr*

The means by which we live have outdistanced the ends for which we live. Our scientific power has outrun our physical power. We have guided missiles and misguided men.
— *Martin Luther King, Jr.*

Whatever the word 'secular' is made to signify in current usage, historically it cannot be equated with worldliness. Modern man, when he lost the certainty of a world to come, was thrown back on himself and not upon this world; far from believing that the world might be potentially immortal, he was not even sure that it was real.
— *Hannah Arendt*

Men become neurotic at the mid-point of life because, in some sense, they have been false to themselves, and have strayed too far from the path which Nature intended them to follow.
— *Anthony Storr (on Jung)*

The world has gone mad today
And day's night today
And black's white today
And wrong's right today .... .
— Cole Porter ('Anything Goes')

Questions ...

In what ways did the discovery of radioactivity upset confidence in the laws of physical science?

What is the Second Law of Thermodynamics and why has it been said that ignorance of it is as much a sign of a limited education as ignorance of Shakespeare or Beethoven?

What is entropy?

In what way does modern physics seem to take us back to a world of illusion and mysterious, unknown forces?

Is there, after all, a 'ghost in the machine'?

When we think of the problems that science has helped to create, would we all be better off with less science?

The end of certainty?

In 1887 the French chemist Berthelot announced: 'From now on there is no mystery about the Universe.' A few years later, Britain's Lord Kelvin proclaimed the impossibility of heavier-than-air flying machines. About the same time the German professor Lippmann told his students: 'physics is a subject that is exhausted ... you had better turn your attention to something else.' Ironically it was in physics that the first cracks began to appear in the scientific establishment, cracks that were to spread, widen, and eventually destroy the image of the cosmos as a vast and intricate, but comprehensible, machine. Despite the efforts of its supporters to push aside growing doubts, the Newtonian world began to crumble as inevitably as the Ptolemaic image of the universe after Copernicus.

The disintegration began with a series of discoveries that pointed to instability in atoms, the very building bricks of the known universe. The mysterious new force, electricity, was found to be corpuscular and the recently discovered cathode rays from certain electrical apparatus were found to be rapid streams of tiny particles of subatomic size. But where did all these particles come from? Then there was the peculiar phenomenon known as radioactivity; certain substances emitted multiple rays, some alpha (α) particles which had a positive electrical charge, some beta (β) particles which were negatively charged, and some gamma (γ) rays which resembled yet another puzzling discovery, X-rays. Ernest Rutherford (1871−1937) suggested that radioactive substances contained unstable elements, the atoms of which were in a continuous state of disintegration; eventually the suspicion was confirmed that all atoms were, more or less, unstable and that they were all composed of smaller particles. Some of these particles were electrons, each weighing one two-thousandth part of a hydrogen atom, and their rapid movement in a solid constituted an electric current. They could be pulled out by high voltages from apparently all substances to form what was previously known as cathode rays, and they were also the β-particles of radioactivity.

Clearly, the atom was not the simple indivisible particle envisaged by Dalton and further experiments by Rutherford indicated the need for a much more complex model. Thin layers of gold were bombarded by accelerated α-particles—bits of atoms from radioactive disintegration; most of these particles passed through the gold with apparently undiminished speeds (could matter be largely 'empty'?), but some particles actually bounced off with increased speed (Figure 8−1). The exercise had been compared with the rapid firing of tiny missiles at insects flying at random inside the dome of a cathedral; the results suggested that the insects were returning some of the missiles like vigorous tennis players! The picture of the atom which began to take shape consisted of a tiny, heavy, positively-charged nucleus surrounded at relatively large distances, like planets around the sun, by electrons. In stable atoms this microcosmic planetary system circulated constantly but radioactive atoms spontaneously broke up like tiny exploding alarm clocks, throwing out an assortment of cog-wheels and springs.

Breakdown of classical scientific laws

In particular, the radioactive element radium constantly produces other substances, including the gaseous element helium; and, in a sealed insulated container, it is found to be constantly at a higher temperature than its surroundings. This behaviour is not accounted for by two fundamental laws of Newtonian science, those of Conservation of Matter and of Energy; a new element is being formed from another element and energy is being created. Two of the

FIGURE 8-1

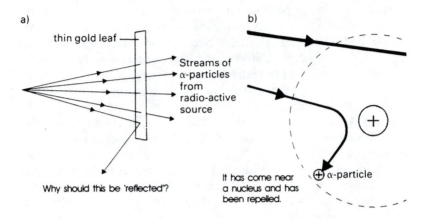

Rutherford's experiments
Most streams of α-particles pass through the gold undeviated; (a). The atom of gold must therefore be relatively empty, but with a positively charged nucleus which repels any α-particles which happen to approach it directly, (b).

cornerstones of nineteenth century science were thus found to be fragile. The early twentieth century scientists must have wondered if they were back in the Dark Ages; Rutherford himself wrote a booklet called *The Newer Alchemy* in which he described transformations, spontaneous or artificial, of one element into another. It had been impossible for the alchemists to turn lead into gold but atomic physics could bring about similar changes by fusing the atoms of one element with bits of another. Rutherford believed that such transformation was possible only on a minute scale; he also stated — only a few decades before Hiroshima — that the relatively large energy changes involved could not be put to use either for bombs or as substitutes for wood, coal, or oil.

British scientists referred to the collisions between these atomic particles as 'subatomic billiards,' but it soon became clear that Newtonian laws of motion and the corresponding mathematics could not accurately predict the speed or direction of these colliding subatomic particles. These older principles are accurate enough for predictions of paths of billiard balls or even of space projectiles but they are as useless to atomic scientists as a large screwdriver in the repair of a digital watch — or, indeed, of a radio telescope. They may *help* — the old laws are not wrong, merely approximate — but they will not even begin to probe the deepest mysteries of the very small or the very large.

The quantum theory and the birth of a new physics

In 1900 Max Planck had introduced his quantum theory, by which energy is regarded not as a continuous stream but as a succession of little packets called *quanta*. At first, scientists were reluctant to accept this idea, regarding it as a useful mathematical device to explain certain problems connected with radiation but without any correspondence to reality. But Einstein, in 1905, used Planck's theory to explain the photoelectric effect (rays of light initiating currents of electricity) and, later, Niels Bohr (1885–1962) showed that the same ideas supported the evolving model of the atom. Scientists soon had no alternative but to accept the quantum theory; they may have objected to a lack of 'common sense' but so had the Earth-centred philosophers when confronted with the Copernican model of the universe.

It was Einstein who first sketched plans for a new physics, just as Copernicus had created the prototype of the Newtonian universe. Unlike Copernicus, Einstein was widely welcomed by those scientists eager to make sense of the increasing chaos of their crumbling world. Many of them, steeped in Newtonian common sense, were even more mystified by the new physics than their seventeenth century counterparts had been by Newton. At least the imaginative Copernican, confronted with the idea of a voyaging, spinning Earth, could cling to the idea of something fixed and absolute in which these terrifying movements occurred. Philosophers might quibble about the nature of this stationary framework (if time is 'like an ever-rolling stream,' what are the banks?) but there surely must be *something*.

Since the acceptance of the idea of light waves, scientists had imagined the existence of an *aether*, a 'substance' which permeated space and in which light waves travel as sound waves travel in air. In a famous experiment of 1881, Michelson and Morley tried to find evidence for the existence of this *aether*. By comparing with a boat travelling in a river they argued that light travelling first with the 'wind' (produced by the rotation of the earth in the stationary *aether*) and then back to its source would take longer than travelling the same distance at right angles to the 'wind.' Their results showed no such difference. Michelson and Morley thus convincingly demonstrated that there was no physical evidence for the existence of the *aether*. Light waves apparently rippled through nothing.

So Einstein faced the problem that nothing in the universe, not

even space, seemed fixed or absolute. In his theories of relativity
he accepted that everything is in a state of flux, that our knowledge of
space or of time depends wholly on our viewpoints, or frames of
reference. Moreover, everything exists in space *and* time; space
and time are inseparable, time is a fourth dimension to our solid,
everyday world and the whole universe must be looked upon as a
space-time continuum. When there are 'lumps' or 'hollows' in this
continuum, objects move away from or towards them; hitherto,
such movements had been explained by gravitational or magnetic
forces mysteriously operating through space. All this is not the
mere replacement of one theoretical idea by another; Einstein's
account of movement in space-time is a metaphor for a happening
that we cannot visualize. As Bertrand Russell says, in a deceptively

FIGURE 8-2   'Flatland'

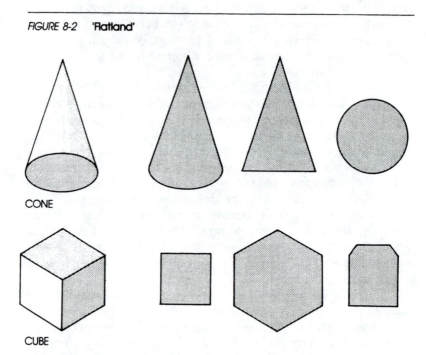

CONE

CUBE

Shadows of solid objects on a flat wall
Familiar objects can produce a variety of shadow shapes depending on their
positions.
    In two-dimensional space, three-dimensional objects would appear to take
on different shapes. The inhabitants of Flatland would see a cone as something
which could appear as any of at least three shapes. If a four-dimensional
creature were to appear in our three-dimensional world we would be equally
startled by its 'magical' changes of appearance.

lucid explanation of relativity, 'I warn the reader not to try to imagine this, as it is impossible.' We are like two-dimensional creatures looking at shadows on their flat world of a cone or a cube in different positions; it seems impossible to them that the different shapes come from the same object (Figure 8−2). They simply cannot *imagine* such an object.

Implications of $E=mc^2$

The full theory of relativity is incomprehensible not only to the layperson but to many scientists, if only because of the impossibility of a full description without much mathematics. But one mathematical equation is both comprehensible and notorious. $E=mc^2$ tells us, first, that there is an equivalence of energy (E) and mass (m), that matter can be transformed into energy, or *vice versa*; in other words, the Laws of Conservation of Matter and of Energy, although separately untrue, are reassuringly valid if regarded as a single law. Secondly, since c is a very large number (it represents the velocity of light), the energy released during the annihilation of even a small amount of matter is enormous. Thirdly, but not so obviously, it is possible to infer from the equation that if we could travel at a velocity approaching that of light, we would age more slowly than people moving at normal speeds; if we could spend a week travelling to distant galaxies we would be a week older on our return to Earth—but the Earth would have aged perhaps by one hundred years.

Science fiction? Certainly this was the reaction even of scientists when the ideas were first crystallized. But the passage of time has made them more acceptable and even provided some proof. There is evidence that, deep in the universe, matter is created by the congealing of energy and we know that small quantities of matter were destroyed in providing the colossal energy necessary for the devastation of Hiroshima and Nagasaki in 1945. When atoms of hydrogen coalesce to form new atoms of helium the result can be the explosion of a hydrogen bomb; or, if the energy can be controlled and released slowly, it can (and eventually will) provide virtually unlimited electrical power. And, although the third consequence of the equation has not yet realized the time-travel dreams of science fiction writers, it is consistent with the strange behaviour of subatomic particles which seem to move in a time-scale quite different from ours.

So far, so disturbing; and, only occasionally, so comforting. In its basic predictability, the new physics offered compensations for some strange new ideas. At first, it seemed to writers like H. G.

Wells that the new ideas were even more liberating than those of Newton. But behind this optimism there lingered doubts based on a warning from the older physics. This was the idea of entropy, incorporated in the famous Second Law of Thermodynamics, which suggests that the universe as a whole is moving inexorably towards total chaos. We may try to reassure ourselves that order does, from time to time, emerge in the growth of a crystal, the blossoming of a flower, the birth of a child; but elsewhere a greater disorder is being created. We are confronted with the gloomy thought that there may seem to be no point in trying to create some order in our lives since the cosmos as a whole is doomed to what has been dramatically described as 'heat death.'

The fantasy world of modern physics

But it is when we look at the most recent implications of quantum mechanics that we begin to realize what it means to have the rational Newtonian ground removed from beneath our feet. In his Principle of Uncertainty, Werner Heisenberg (born 1901) showed that it is impossible to know precisely what is happening inside an atom; the very act of investigating one feature may disturb another, so that all we can hope to establish is the probability, not the certainty, of the atom's behaviour. The idea has led to mathematical principles which make the behaviour comprehensible to the scientist; it has helped to explain why certain elements interact, why some substances conduct electricity, why and in what circumstances nuclear energy is available, and what happens in the 'black holes' of the universe. But it also introduces the possibility that bits of atoms can literally appear from nowhere, or exist in two places at once; that the atom itself, not the model, may be a figment of our imagination; that the 'real' world is one of millions of coexisting worlds each impossible to visit from another; that we, as observers, actually create the universe as we contemplate it. Small wonder that physics, to some minds, has acquired the mystical aura that used to be associated with religions of the Far East.

This is worse than finding ourselves back at 'square one.' We thought that we had made ourselves independent of mysticism; when Einstein said 'God does not play dice' he was expressing faith in the power of science to discover rational solutions to nature's problems. We had carefully designed the scientific box of tools to reveal an intricate but ordered universe capable of being understood by our intricate and ordered minds. But the physics which Einstein initiated has exposed a universe of fantasy in which there seems to be no place for the rational, a realm of nonsense in which it is even more nonsensical to employ the tools of reason. We begin to sympathize with Don Quixote, proud of a well-tested lance, in conflict not with a monster, not even with a windmill, but with a shimmering mirage for which his lance is useless. And it is no longer a matter of adjusting the imagination — a painful but healthy process which man, from the time of Copernicus at least, has increasingly had to experience. The new physics goes beyond the limits of what we can imagine; as Sir James Jeans put it, 'not only is the universe queerer than we supposed but it is queerer than we can suppose.'

Scientific confusion reflected in the 'real' world

If we turn away from the cosmos and the physics of subatomic particles to what we used to think of as the real world, we find little comfort. Apparently intoxicated by our success in exploiting nature, we seem hell-bent on poisoning the planet not only by pumping noxious substances into the sea and sky but by burning up natural means of neutralizing such substances. We may console ourselves with occasional scientific and social victories for reason. We experience surges of hope when we see the political changes in Europe and Africa but these increasingly seem to be mere oases in a widening desert of ignorance and superstition which is all the more dangerous because it is often concealed by pseudo-scientific camouflage. Many sophisticates of today openly acknowledge a debt to their astrologers; some American politicians have become 'born again Christians' and, in their newly discovered fundamentalist enthusiasm, seek to ban the teaching of Darwin's theory; earnest campaigners against 'junk' foods and nuclear fuel often base their message not on informed opinion but on woolly, mystical views of the benefits of nature in the raw. There is now a positive hunger for what have been described as 'the comforts of unreason.' Even science itself seems to have been infected; the very titles of scientific books like *The Tao of Physics* or *The Dancing Wu-Li Masters* suggest that modern physics owes less to reason than to mysticism.

Our forefathers in the nineteenth century saw in science the promise of a brave, new world in which reason, and presumably wisdom, would prevail. Having apparently failed in this promise, it is now in popular disrepute. Admittedly, modern medicine prolongs life, relieves pain, and continues to control nature; but that life which is prolonged seems to filled with money-making and pleasure-seeking. It is obsessed with sex rather than love; it equates success with popularity not with quality; it is increasingly anarchic in the absence of any authority to which it might be responsible. God has already been removed from this position of authority and the science which has been put in God's place seems to be inadequate.

To writers like Franz Kafka (1883–1924), the world around us has simply become a frightening reflection of a meaningless cosmos. *The Trial* and *The Castle* evoke a nightmare atmosphere which distorts rationality in a disturbing parody of the world's absurdities. Thinking humans are doomed to lose themselves in a crazy limbo which, from time to time, shows a tantalizing resemblance to a 'real' world in which millions of people starve while surplus food is destroyed elsewhere, and where governments accumulate enough weapons to destroy themselves and their enemies several times over. Kafka's world and our own have merged into a dreamlike state no longer involved with the reasoning and practicalities of classical science; we believe what we want to believe, we indulge our personal and political prejudices by reference to the pseudo-sciences of Freudians or Marxists and turn a deaf ear to those who remind us that these beliefs are mere distortions. Indeed, some of us retort that all beliefs, particularly those founded on classical science, are illusions; we therefore adopt a philosophy of nihilism in which 'anything goes' or, in turning to more and more bizarre beliefs, reinforce the cynical view that the new Dark Age has already begun. Recalling the reaction of John Donne to the demise of the old cosmic image (page 95), we find a parallel sentiment from W. B. Yeats (1865–1939):

> *Things fall apart; the centre cannot hold;*
> *Mere anarchy is loosed upon the world.*

Despair of the individual

If, tempted by the attitude of Voltaire's hero Candide, we decide to ignore the world and its problems and 'cultivate our own garden,' we look in vain for comfort. Technology has provided tranquillizers for easy escape from reality—a more appropriate palliative than the aspirin which would remove headaches caused by problem solving—and behaviourist psychology has discovered how, literally, to change our minds. But at what cost to our individualities? Each of us begins gloomily to accept a role as a mere constituent of 'the masses,' a unit in sociological or psychological statistics. Jung parted company with Freud because he felt that Freudian methods were too coldly scientific; what would he think of modern trends in the study of the mind? And in any case, did not his own psychology, with its emphases on primitive mythology and poetical symbolism, end up in the same mystical fog that characterizes both modern physics and ancient religions?

But why not? The world around us is largely illusion; we have begun to accept that atoms themselves are largely empty space in which, if the nucleus were placed over central London, the outer shell of electrons would hover somewhere close to Brighton. Berkeley warned us that the solidity of matter was as illusory as that of a spinning bicycle wheel; and even if, like Dr Johnson, we choose to ignore such philosophical speculation, we cannot ignore a similar image which shows the circle of destruction, radiating out to Brighton, caused by a nuclear bomb exploded over central London.

We have convinced ourselves that nothing is certain except the inexorable drift of the universe towards total chaos. There is no stable truth, no fixed standard of behaviour. The idea of relativity has persuaded us to bend our moral codes so that old laws like 'thou shall not kill' have become blurred by clauses beginning with 'except when ...' or 'unless ....' We continue to educate our children in the traditional way, either in science or in the arts, aware that neither path will lead them to a full appreciation of the truth but dimly hopeful that they may ultimately find lucrative jobs and, perhaps, some distraction from the more obvious personal and social problems. We have realized that, in the heady progression of science away from superstition and the supernatural, we have managed to separate emotion from reason, love from sex, spirit from body. (A recent Muslim reaction to sex education in British schools aptly underlines this; some Muslim parents claim that there is too much about contraception and the mechanics of sex and not enough about emotions, morality, and family life.) Many of us can no longer return to that 'old-fashioned' religion which tried to blend the science of its day with a supernatural plan for mankind. But have we tried to put anything in place of that religion? It not, we might look to this spiritual under-nourishment for clues to what is wrong with our emotional lives and seek causes for the disillusionment which we have allowed science to create.

Unlike those scientific pioneers of the nineteenth century who replaced their faith in old beliefs with a way of thought which, for them, pointed the way more clearly to truth, we find ourselves completely disorientated. Not only are we bewildered about the choice of various paths to truth; we wonder if the goal is worth seeking, or even if it is real. In his poem, *The Oxen*, Thomas Hardy recalls a childhood myth, that oxen 'on Christmas Eve at twelve of the clock' knelt down on the straw of their shed. Admitting that few people in modern times would accept such a fancy, Hardy describes how he would eagerly go back to the scenes of his childhood, to investigate the myth, 'hoping it might be so.' Our problem is that, deep down, we have learned that it cannot be so.

CHAPTER NINE

Integration

Science is spectrum analysis; art is photosynthesis.
— *K. Kraus*

We have art that we may not perish from truth.
— *Nietzsche*

The truth indeed has never been preached by the Buddha, seeing that one has to realize it within oneself.
— *Sutra Lamkara*

The union of the mathematician with the poet, fervour with measure, passion with correctness, this surely is the ideal.
— *William James*

If one advances confidently in the direction of his dreams, and endeavours to live the life which he has imagined, he will meet with a success unexpected in common hours ... In proportion as he simplifies himself, the laws of the universe will appear less complex ... If you have built castles in the air, your work need not be lost; that is where they should be. Now put the foundations under them.
— *H. D. Thoreau*

Much human pleasure and fulfilment, as well as creative achievement, come from solitude. This is in accord with many religious messages: the kingdom of heaven is within, the god within and the inner explorations of Buddhism.
— *Anthony Storr*

Because there is no cosmic point to the life that each of us perceives on this distant bit of dust at galaxy's edge, all the more reason for us to maintain in proper balance what we have here. Because there is nothing else. This is it. And quite enough, all in all.
— *Gore Vidal*

Education to-day, more than ever before, must see clearly the dual objectives: education for living and educating for making a living.
— *James Mason Wood*

The best of the stories are realistic and paint life as it is, but because every line is permeated, as with a juice, by an awareness of purpose, you feel, besides life as it is, also life as it ought to be, and this captivates you.
— *Graham Greene on Chekhov*

Know thyself.
— *Anon (written up in the temple at Delphi)*

Questions . . .

Can there be any certainty in uncertainty? Is the Uncertainty Principle another example of an apparent scientific weakness actually being a strength?

Is there anything new in the idea of increasing universal disorder? What do we do about it?

Is it possible to accept both myth and science? poetry and psychology? faith and critical doubt? science and religion?

To what extent does normal education separate these topics? Should it do so?

Do we passively accept too much in education? How much should we be allowed to discover for ourselves? How much should we be allowed to criticize?

What sort of religion could a scientist accept?

What has science, the history and philosophy of science, to offer the majority of us who are not scientists?

'Humankind cannot bear much reality.'
The neurotic builds castles in the air, the
psychotic lives in them.'
In the present world turmoil, is escape from reality the only way to happiness?

Contemporary distrust of science is not new

'A multitude of causes, unknown to former times, are now acting with a combined force to blunt the discriminating power of the mind and, unfitting it for voluntary exertion, to reduce it to a state of almost savage torpor. The most effective of these causes are the great national events which are daily taking place, and the increasing accumulation of men in cities, where the uniformity of their occupations produces a craving for extraordinary incident, which the rapid communication of intelligence hourly gratifies.' So wrote the poet William Wordsworth in 1798 — two centuries before our own age of drug abuse, widespread pornography, X-rated videos, punk rock and soap operas which many people find more attractive than reality; and at a time when Europe was only just beginning to be enveloped in a haze of industrial pollution.

Ours is not the first age to distrust scientific thought and, while enjoying its material benefits, to rebel against its cold inhumanity. But the pessimism of today is more profound. The power of nuclear weapons, the spread of industrial pollution, the increased rate of burning of fossil fuels, all seem to bring nearer a worldwide catastrophe, even global annihilation. Furthermore, even if we manage to combine the world's intellectual and technical resources to avert all this, we are left with the one scientific certainty in a whole skein of uncertainties, that the universe is eventually doomed to 'heat death' — when, according to a thermodynamical law, energy will no longer be available for conversion into useful work. Thus, if the world is not to end in a sudden bang, it will expire with a long whimper; we are therefore tempted to give up the struggle, to reflect that the idea of global and individual progress to perfection through science was never more than a dream. In such circumstances superstition appeals. We read about apparently intelligent people seeking peace, harmony, and higher states of consciousness in ten-metre-high wooden pyramids, who claim to think best when their heads point south, and who believe that 'London has an extraordinarily high density of chakra points, where two or more paths of psychic energy converge.'

But if there is nothing new in a drift towards the irrational, it is reassuring to know that the work of scientists continues to move stubbornly in the opposite direction. Science seeks to create order from disorder, to find some rational meaning in the apparently meaningless, to oppose the natural tendency towards chaos. Scientists accept uncertainty and attempt to limit it. They use their imaginations to create simplified images of the unknown and set out to find how closely those images resemble reality. They say, in effect: let us proceed as if the horizons are clear and our destination certain; let us find out, by trial and error, how far we can safely and successfully go. They may find that they cannot finish the journey, that the destination is a mirage; but the world they have explored has become a little clearer, they now have a reasonably reliable sketch-map for confident travel in a wider area. In proceeding *as if* there were absolute truths to discover, they have created not a retreat from reality but an observatory from which to plan their next moves.

The value to the individual of the scientific method

In behaving as if our world is a safe and predictable place, we are thus taking an example from science. In planning our careers, for example, we do not (certainly should not) set our sights on single goals which may be extremely difficult to reach; we take into account the possible uncertainties and, bearing in mind various acceptable alternatives, we widen the goal and thus increase our chance of success. In fact, we are applying the Principle of Uncertainty whereby a circle, in the representation of an atom, represents not the fixed orbit of an electron but the extent of a more diffuse region where the electron will most probably be.

When we seem to ignore the prophecy of ultimate doom for planet Earth (and, indeed, for our own individual lives) and strive to create some sort of dignified order in our lives, we are again following the scientist's lead. In encouraging the widening view that the earlier fate of Earth is in our hands, we act as if the world around us is perfectible and that the recent tendency towards increasing decay is reversible. We show, as one wit put it, that 'we believe in life before death.'

The need for popular control of technology

It is impossible to think of any scientific advance, from the discovery of fire to the liberation of atomic energy, that cannot be used either for benefit to humankind or for harm. Early in this century the ingenuity of German chemists, Fritz Haber and Karl Bosch, made it possible to combine the elements in air and water to produce explosives, at a time when Germany was deprived of conventional raw materials from South America. This process prolonged the first World War, but, in a world guided by reason and compassion, it could also provide tons of cheap fertilizer which could make Third World hunger a thing of the past (Figure 9-1).

This is why it is imperative for all of us to understand the implications of scientific and technological issues. Only by understanding can we hope to control the scientific machine and to have control over our own world. If cynics remind us that, in the face of inevitable chaos, we are wasting our time, we can remind them that nothing is certain, that our striving may well create one of -those oases of certainty in an otherwise desolate universe. If they

FIGURE 9-1

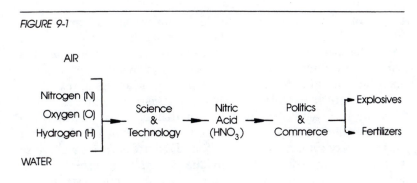

The Haber Process
Science makes it possible to combine the three elements. But the choice of the end product is not decided by the scientist.

further warn us that the science which effected so much change in past centuries is a mere approximation of the fantasy which modern science has become, we can retort that this is no reason for discarding the familiar science. I remember, as a young graduate involved for the first time with problems of industry, hearing the views of a less qualified but more experienced colleague: 'When you young people meet everyday problems you drag out your Schrodinger and your quantum mechanics, you argue and you get into a real mess; as for me, I never got beyond Dalton and his billiard-ball atoms — but I get on with the job. I solve the problems and you don't.' In my opinion, and for this problem, this man took the right attitude and the right intellectual tools and he also used them skilfully and succesfully, with scientific common sense.

Lessons to be learned from non-scientists

But the problems are undeniably huge and it is tempting for the individual to give up the struggle both against mass opinion and the forces of nature. William Wordsworth tried to show the way towards a philosophy of life which accepted the materialism of the first scientific revolution but did not ignore the loneliness of the individual nor the new fear of ultimate extinction. He believed that it is possible for each of us to create a rich inner life, to translate the sad loneliness into a 'bliss of solitude,' to replace the dread of death by a deeper appreciation of the glories of life. For him, the route to this awareness was through poetry, 'in emotion recollected in tranquillity'; for others it might be through fiction or music or art. In our own times the individual who wishes to experience a full 'life before death' may be encouraged by the romantic, though somewhat depressing, existentialism of Albert Camus or Jean-Paul Sartre; they came to the conclusion that individuals must create their own purposes for living and their own meanings for existence in a life which has otherwise come to seem meaningless. They lived in a very different world from that of Wordsworth, when order, certainty, and progress seemed guaranteed by Newton. Yet it was that very confidence which inspired science to reveal a universe which gradually reduced the individual to a frightened speck — even before the arrival, on the scientific scene, of Albert Einstein.

What can the individual do?

It is ironic that Einstein, who was to replace the certainties and optimism of the Newtonian model of the universe, was initially attracted to science because it seemed to offer a structured and purposeful refuge for the bewildered individual from the irrationalities and moral failures of the world. He admired such individual scientists as Marie Curie — her purity of will, her austerity, her objectivity, her incorruptible judgments, above all her role as a servant of society. But he also found inspiration in fiction, particularly that of the great Russian novelist Fyodor Dostoevsky.

Dostoevsky was concerned with the fate of the individual in society — not, it must be emphasized, the fate of the 'average man' who is a statistical creation representing in miniature the behaviour of society as a whole. The individual may be a 'loner,' a 'drop out,' a dissident who does not travel with the crowd and whose views and needs tend to vanish within the statistics. Yet a successful social system must ensure the happiness of every individual whether that individual is fated to live life in obscurity or, occasionally, to emerge as a leader who will alter forever the lives of large sections of society. In his search for social harmony, Dostoevsky was able to imagine a synthesis of two divergent trains of thought, one concerned with the rigid, classical reason inspired by Newtonian science and the other with the rebellious, irrational forces of nature which do not conform with the behaviour of civilized society.

Einstein claimed that Dostoevsky gave him 'more than any other thinker.' Certainly, one can see parallels between his scientific work and Dostoevsky's literary conclusions. Einstein, too, made a synthesis by which the fixed framework of Newtonian science was to be seen as an approximation of a wider, more fluid and more nebulous system. Newton's Laws are still accurate enough to put a human on the moon, even if they cannot give precise accounts of the vastness of space or of the behaviour of sub-atomic particles. Probability may now have replaced certainty and truth must now be seen as relative, but within the narrow bounds of everyday human events, former 'certainties' and 'absolute truths' could still seem unchanged. Einstein was able to satisfy himself, and to assure the rest of us, that harmony was still possible, at least on a small scale, even if the universe as a whole was no longer quite as simple as it had previously appeared.

At the same time, the Einsteinian view, being less rigid, less confining than the Newtonian, can liberate us from traditional, dogmatic thinking and encourage us to explore new and more imaginative approaches to problems. It does not abandon traditional methods of problem solving; it simply reminds us that they have their limits in both application and scale. We have to learn, yet again, that it is the restless, probing, even shifting search for truth which characterizes science and not the 'truths' which the search occasionally discovers. We must always remind ourselves that we will never reach the ultimate truth; all that we can hope to do is to improve those maps and models which help us to proceed, cautiously but confidently, on the way.

The value to the individual of a scientific attitude

It is this 'old-fashioned,' *well*-fashioned scientific method that should be our most cherished gift from science and not the approximations to truth that eventually become scientific dogma. It applies not only to science even in the broadest sense; it has helped to change views in a wide range of human thought from art criticism to politics. Karl Popper has pointed out that, whatever problems we consider, the idea of falsification leading to the discovery of what is wrong, enables us to proceed more surely in the direction of what must be right. It also persuades us to put our trust in what is seen to work rather than in attractive theories which do not stand up to practical tests. It reminds us that criticism, of both our own ideas and those who seek to influence us, is not to be avoided but to be positively sought, so that the ideas may be scrutinized, tested, and ultimately improved. Above all, it teaches us to distrust those who claim to be certain about their beliefs and to transform a healthy scepticism into confidence in our ability to deal with fresh problems. It gives new meaning to the term 'free will' and it also reminds us of our dependence on others and the need to take into account both their opinions and well-being.

Spiritual hunger of the individual

But one can solve many of life's problems, one's conscience may
be clear about responsibilities to other people and to the planet,
and one can still feel ill at ease with oneself. The idea persists that
science is not enough; those two paths to truth still diverge. There
is still that polarization of reason and emotion, the intellect and the
spirit, which may split our own view of life and which may even
explain dichotomies of behaviour in different societies at different
times. In recent times we have only to remember the contrast
between intellectual achievements of Germany and Japan and the
atrocities of wartime concentration camps. 'The soul of man is
naturally religious,'says Laurens van der Post in a book on Jung; 'It
gives a man hunger greater than any physical hunger. If this
hunger is not satisfied, men and their societies either wither or
perish in some disaster unconsciously brought down on themselves.'

The trouble is that many of us have ceased to believe in the
traditional messages of religion. In our scientific age, the idea of
God as a creator or father-figure is dismissable as superstition. In
the face of our experience of science, to go back to such simplistic
beliefs seems like a return to the Dark Ages. Science has beautifully
shaped our ability to reason and to cease to use it, even worse to
misuse it, is tantamount to a crime.

Here again, science indicates a possible solution. The idea of
God can be viewed as a metaphor, a model which is not the whole
truth but which helps us to understand some of the mysteries of
the truth. Some of us may never go beyond this idea; we may be
content to remain within the Newtonian approximations to truth
rather than to venture into the wider Einsteinian world. Neither
course is wrong; neither course can be completely right. Those
following each course act *as if* their map is the whole truth; danger
arises only if they begin to assume that it *is* the whole truth.

Thus, to some, God may be a fatherly creator whom we displease
if we destroy the Earth and its inhabitants, all of which he has
provided. To others, the Earth is a single, live, complex unit called
Gaia (after a Greek goddess) who operates to stabilize the Earth.
So, if we pollute the seas and the atmosphere, Gaia will react to try
to absorb or cancel these changes. If we persist with the pollution,
Gaia's reaction may be too slow to avoid widespread, irreversible
destruction of life. Either belief or model will show us the way to a
sane, sensible harmony with nature; but the way will be found by
human efforts inspired by the chosen model, not by supernatural
activity of the model itself. When the model begins to be regarded
as anything more than a convenient fiction, its users have already
begun to slacken their efforts and superstition begins to take over.

Are religious differences simply differences of language?

Different religions provide different models. The differences between them and between their different sects are often mere differences in language. The answer to the question, Do you believe in God? can have only one answer: it depends what you mean by God. Some people find it convenient to think of a God 'out there' in space; others think of the 'God within' representing the highest, noblest aspirations of the human spirit, manifest not only in humanitarian works but in works of art. Either view can initiate changes for good in the world around us. But, as Jonathan Schell (in his book *The Abolition*) has said' 'If the inner landscapes of our souls do not change, the outer landscape of the world will not change either.' Such a thought makes sense not only of Christ's statement that the Kingdom of Heaven is within us, but of his exhortation to put the love of God (within) above the love of our fellows.

How the individual spiritual hunger may be satisfied

We have come to the heart of the matter. Most of us are not capable of changing the world even if we want to, but we all want to improve those private worlds which matter more to us than the wider world of nature; and, as Jonathan Schell has hinted, there is also something positively unselfish about that. Indeed, there is not much point in living in an improved wider world if those small human problems persist or even, because we choose to ignore them, intensify. That splitting apart of the intellect and spirit is an old problem; 'all work and no play . . . .' and 'man does not live by bread alone' tell the same story. We have even got scientific evidence for it; those tests on astronauts, about to spend many lonely hours in space, showed that physical, as well as mental health deteriorates if one is not allowed to dream. Too much concentration on examinations or getting ahead in the rat-race of business, diminishing time outside of these activities for anything more emotionally demanding than television, can lead to depression. If we try to suppress a need for some sort of fantasy in our waking lives we either suffer or find dubious relief by methods which aggravate, rather than cure, the condition.

It may seem ironic that our scientific path into the unknown has led to a truth so multi-faceted that we have been forced to create an integrated image of intellect and emotion which looks all too familiar. Voltaire said, 'If God did not exist, it would be necessary to invent him.' Has our path brought us back full circle? Well, yes and no; that is how some people may choose to describe it. But we have certainly returned to the message of Jung who passionately maintained that the human mind must be 'whole' if the personality is to be well-balanced, healthy, and happy. This 'wholeness' is not the result of a synthesis of two separate parts but the integration of something which was naturally whole but has been split by experience. The Yin-Yang symbol is particularly appropriate because, like two faces of the same coin, one part does not properly exist without the other. We simply have to learn to respond to the demands of both and to beware of any scheme, particularly in formal education, which effectively seeks to develop one part of our minds to the neglect and atrophy of the other.

Parallel between education and the scientific method

We have to recognize that much of our education is a form of scientific method. I watch my one-year-old granddaughter trying to co-ordinate the growing strength of her muscles with her awareness of the world around her. She has a problem, how to reach an inaccessible toy; she vaguely forms an idea about how the problem might be solved; she takes tentative action, moves towards the toy, overbalances; she revises her plan and tries again. She finds that each new trial benefits from the errors of her former attempts. Later, her intellectual development follows the same pattern, a pattern of trial and error recently glorified by the name *cybernetics*, 'the science of control and communication in the animal and the machine.' It is a pattern which all of us employ when we are struggling to master a new manual or mental skill; it involves logical reasoning, imagination, and the practical testing of hypotheses; when it sheds hypotheses which do not survive the test of experience, it illustrates a lesson of Karl Popper. It is a process which is continually being refined and modified by changing circumstances.

Notice that the child's actions are all that we see; once again, we resemble those philosophers watching scientific work through the window of a laboratory. We may deduce the workings of the child's mind from her actions but we cannot so easily estimate the importance of her emotional background. If she feels secure in this background she will show more confidence in herself. But we can recognize her pleasure when she discovers solutions to her problems; it is the same joy of discovery that we experience when we are led by a skilful teacher to find solutions to mathematical problems, or by an author or dramatist to unravel for ourselves the tangled complication of a plot or of a personality. We feel frustrated if we are simply told the solutions, if the plot is baldly stated rather than suggested. Einstein has described the experience in terms of problem solving in science, but the sentiments apply equally well to the delights of discovery in fiction or drama: 'The final results appear almost simple; any intelligent undergraduate can understand them without much trouble. But the years of searching in the dark for a truth that one feels, but cannot express; the intense desire and the alternation of confidence and misgiving, until one breaks through to clarity and understanding, are only known to him who has himself experienced them.'

Inadequacy of traditional education

Ironically, the rarity of this experience is a main reason for the inadequacy of much science education. Teaching techniques and textbooks can clarify, simplify, exemplify to such an extent that the essential mystery evaporates. When pupils are encouraged to find out for themselves, the aim of the search is often so clear and discovery so structured that individual initiative and originality of thought are minimised; there is little time for doubt, criticism, or lengthy investigation of alternative hypotheses. School syllabuses being so overloaded, this compression and cutting of corners is inevitable and even necessary; imaginative syllabuses (or imaginative treatment of more old-fashioned syllabuses) lose their power to enthral. The would-be scientist is given an entirely false picture of the subject; the belief is implanted that science is a collection of established facts, principles, and solutions which can be mastered by those with sufficient enthusiasm and persistence. In being involved mainly with the verification of textbook topics students will be denied the delight of trying to provide their own solutions. Furthermore, since solutions once discovered often seem obvious, today's budding scientist may well form the impression that scientists of the past were somewhat dim-witted.

Meanwhile, a bewildered majority is having a prejudice confirmed; science is clearly the esoteric activity of a white-coated band of eccentrics. This classroom segregation is partly due to pressure to create more scientists, partly due to the mistaken zeal (or narrow outlook?) of over-specialized science teachers who are unwilling or unable to devote time to wider implications of a topic, or to alternative hypotheses which they know to be 'wrong.' The non-scientific majority eventually specializes in history, art, or literature but with, at best, a distorted view of how the progress of science has interacted with the development of its chosen subjects. It is not uncommon to find a sixth-form historian unable to write more than a few lines on the effect of Newton's work on history;

or to discover that an undergraduate who wishes to study Chaucer or Shakespeare has little idea of the revolutionary changes in scientific thought which took place between the lifetimes of these writers. Eventually this half-educated majority will augment a scientifically illiterate majority in society, a majority which is dependent on science and technology but distrustful of its power and yet unable to criticize it with any confidence.

From time to time new thinking about the school curriculum tries to remedy the faults; it attempts to encourage learning by discovery and open up new fields for study — science and society, the effect of scientific discovery on literature, the interplay between science and history, the ways in which science determines our patterns of life and thought. But the exciting prospects for the satisfaction of individual interests and skills tend to dwindle, in the packed timetable of an average school day, to formulae for passing the necessary examinations. As T. H. Huxley (champion of Darwin) put it: Students work to pass, not to know ... They do pass and they don't know.' Only when syllabuses are pruned of much factual content, only when examinations are able to encourage individual approaches both to scientific problems and to related fields of study will the scientific wood be clearer than the separate trees. Obviously examination candidates must have a minimum fund of scientific knowledge but, unless this is set within a framework of appreciation of scientific method it is no more (or no less) important than a dictionary to a writer. It is the skill in making use of the knowledge, not the knowledge itself, which matters. That is why an ideal education would be less concerned with the facts and techniques of test tube chemistry, rat dissection, and the electrical peculiarities of transistors than with the role of science as the *primum mobile* in the critical investigation of wider problems, both inside and outside the classroom.

Imagination and the art of teaching

It is, of course, in the classroom and not in the examination hall that any educational scheme will succeed or fail. Science teachers must remind themselves that the art of teaching is not so much concerned with the transmission and clarification of information as with persuading the pupil to want to learn; they must resist the urge to push their most alert pupils as quickly as possible towards 'the really interesting stuff'; they must be content occasionally to allow the pupil to take a wrong path. Like actors who have written their own scripts, they must create an active co-operation with their audience by the use of suggestion rather than direct statement, by allowing the pupil to discover the solution rather than be told; they must acquire 'the technique of knowing and yet appearing not to know.' Clearly pupils cannot re-discover all the solutions of the past but they can appreciate the methods of discovery with a selected few, if their imaginations are allowed ample living room and are not stifled by an accumulation of facts whose proper place is in the reference book.

Aims of an integrated education

In these circumstances science students will be more likely to criticize than to memorize, to approach real understanding rather than familiarity with text-book solutions. They will be concerned with the development of ideas and will therefore demand to know something about the history of science. That will not only supply a human face to their studies but will begin to clarify the effect of science on the history of thought, in political and artistic fields as well as in philosophy. The science course would become the Yin of an integrated education.

But we do not yet live in an ideal world. Nonetheless students might more closely approach it as, supplied with a common intellectual framework, they begin to furnish it according to their own individual tastes for science, for history, for literature. The result will be their own unique observatory for an individual view of life and the world. They will not neglect Voltaire's advice and fail 'to cultivate the garden'; their framework will also be a centre for the blossoming of the emotions and the spirit, so that the distinction between the artifice of the framework and the organic growth is increasingly blurred. As more imaginative and humane scientists, or as historians, business people, politicans, artisans, or shopkeepers with a deeper awareness of the implication of science in everyday affairs, they will be more critical of the world around them and better equipped intellectually to cope with its problems. They will become members of society which, perhaps, preserves the illusion of stability in a turbulent universe and which clings to a mere image of truth in a world where no absolute truth exists; but at least their points of view are less distorted than they were and they are in better positions to assess the value of the illusion or the image. And if, ultimately, these ideas are revealed as empty and ephemeral, they may have the satisfaction of knowing that they strove to maintain an oasis of sanity in an expanding desert, that they chose to defy the doom-laden laws of nature instead of living and dying in apathy.

Epilogue

In York Minster, on a cold December afternoon when the weak sunshine barely managed to illuminate the glory of the stained glass windows, I heard a woman visitor whisper, 'It makes you wish you could be a believer again.'

I saw what she meant. The soaring grandeur of the Minster, the awed hush in the gloom, the feeling of what Wordsworth called 'a presence that disturbs me with the joy of elevated thoughts,' all evoked, deep in our minds, those resonances which we equate with religious experience.

But let us not forget, as we admire the lofty magnificence of European cathedrals, that this architectural splendour is based on the imagination and artistic vision of a few forgotten men and executed by the simple scientific skills of countless other human beings. When we contrast their achievement with the relative poverty of their daily lives we find it difficult to avoid phrases like 'dedication to the glory of God.' If we choose to describe the experience in more secular terms we are not trying to depreciate the sense of wonder or reverence; we are not dismissing that feeling of mystery which disturbs us when we are surrounded by these splendid links with the past. We are simply using different language.

Neither let us forget that pride in the exercise of human skills, awareness of beauty, and joy in creativity are not things of the past. When, some years ago, York Minster was struck by lightning, much loving care and painstaking work were directed to its restoration. This involved the same sort of techniques which had already been developed when the Minster was being built more than five hundred years ago. A television documentary about the restoration successfully revealed the feelings of pride in the achievement of various contributing craftsmen. They did not use the same terms as the speakers at the official ceremony; they might have been embarrassed by words like 'beauty' or 'art' — yet it was very clear that they had been ennobled by their experience and we, in our turn, were enriched by listening to them. We did not have to be 'believers' to be deeply affected by man's ability to feel wonder in the creation of beauty. Like Wordsworth, we may find the 'sense sublime' within the 'still, sad music of humanity.'

Ironically, the damage to York Minster was said to have been indirectly caused by opinions similar to those which I have just expressed. The Bishop of Durham has been worried for some time that the Church's insistence on the literal truth of such ideas as the miraculous nature of Christ's birth and resurrection may deter those would-be Christians who prefer to think of these events as symbolic. Some of the Bishop's critics claimed that the lightning damage to York Minster was a sign of God's displeasure with what they claimed was blasphemy. Yet, to many viewers, the television account of the restoration implicitly revealed that the work, when described in terms of human creativity, was just as moving, inspired, and inspiring as when it was depicted in conventional religious terms. It therefore hinted that the Bishop's worry is well-founded, that all of us seek enrichment by what some choose to call religious experience but which others prefer to see as appreciation of beauty either in nature or in art. Once again, is not the difference a mere difference of language?

In reflecting upon his relentless need to compose music, Aaron Copland equated it with the urge to express his feelings about life. 'But why is the job never done? Why must one always begin again? The reason is that each added work brings with it an element of self-discovery. I must create in order to know myself.' We cannot all build cathedrals or compose music but we are all involved with creativity. We have seen that we learn much from science — from the earliest trial-and-error activities of our childhoods to the sophistication of Karl Popper's philosophy — in coping with the creations of work, of hobbies, of family, of our very lives. But even though we may be critical of the psyche as anything more substantial than a scientist's model, we must not be deaf to its demands if we are to maintain that wholeness of mind which, as heaven, Nirvana, or inner peace, Jung has urged us to seek.

Chronological Table

It will be obvious that this table does not attempt to be exhaustive. It lists some of the discoveries and events mentioned in the text simply to provide a perspective for the reader. Its many gaps may be a positive advantage if they are filled with details of individual interests in both the scientific and non-scientific fields.

Fuller biographical details may be found in Asimov's *Biographical Encyclopedia of Science and Technology* while Walter Shepherd's *Outline History of Science* will provide a more comprehensive account of the main discoveries.

B.C.

3000–1400	Minoan civilization in Crete
2800–1700	Pyramids built
c 2300	Chinese astronomers calculated length of year as $365\frac{1}{4}$ days
c 1000	Iron Age settlements in Europe
c 600	Spread of Buddhism Thales of Miletus was one of the first Europeans to study nature without reference to superstition.
c 500	Pythagoras of Samos made a 'religion' from his mystical view of mathematics but many of his discoveries, though based on mysticism, prompted further investigation (later) in a more rational manner

	Empedocles (c. 444) introduced the idea of four elements. Hippocrates founded a medical school, practising medicine in a down-to-earth practical way, without mysticism The Parthenon in Athens was built about this time
c 400	Plato: *Republic* Aristotle: *Ethics* and *Politics*
c 270	Aristarchus' concept of a sun-centred universe.
c 250	Archimedes of Syracuse was one of the greatest mathematicians ever, and one of the greatest engineers of the ancient world
c 240	The Chinese observed what was later to be called Halley's Comet
c 100	Mary the Jewess refined the alembic for distillation

0–1000 A.D.

	The plough introduced to Britain by the Romans
c 100	Hero invented a steam engine using the principles of jet propulsion Greek alchemists already well advanced in purification techniques
c 150	Ptolemy finalized his earth-centred system of the universe
c 170	Galen's views on the circulation of the blood
c 400	St. Augustine's work attempted to confirm Scripture by science
c 500	Silk manufacture introduced to Europe from China Few scholars in the Christian world studied science but the monk Cassiodorus completed a scientific encyclopedia that awakened some scientific curiosity
c 700	Rise of Arabian alchemy

c 800   First-known printed book in China
                 Salerno school of medicine founded
                 The Arabs acquired all mathematical knowledge of
                 the Greeks and proceeded to add to it
                 Al-Nazzam, an Arabic philosopher, suggested bio-
                 logical evolution

c 900   Paper introduced to Europe

c 940   Shen Kua in China made the first artificial magnet

c 970   Al-Khazini used mechanics to test mathematical
                 theorems

1000 A.D.– 1500 A.D.

1074   Omar Khayyam (poet and astronomer) devised a
                 calendar accurate to within one day in 5000 years
                 Compasses and charts in use for navigation

c. 1250   Albertus Magnus, who studied at Padua, revived
                 interest in Aristotle

1263   Roger Bacon explained the rainbow; used lenses to
                 help weak sight; in theory, devised a telescope and
                 magic lantern (But he also believed that lead could
                 be transformed into gold.)
                 Gunpowder now in use in warfare
                 Thomas Aquinas successfully blended Aristotle's
                 philosophy with Christian teachings to provide an
                 influence on the church which persists to the present

1325   William of Occam's 'razor'
                 Clockwork introduced to Europe from China
                 Guns now a feature of warships

1450   Movable type now in use printing
                 Voyages of Columbus, Cabot, de Gama

The sixteenth century

                 Leonardo da Vinci studying mechanics, geology,
                 anatomy

1520   Paracelsus, an alchemist and doctor, sought to free
                 science from superstition (Although he believed
                 that bodily processes were governed by 'spirits' he
                 did much to advance simple medicine.)

1543	Copernicus' theory of the universe Vesalius' researches in anatomy
1576	Tycho Brahe founded an observatory in Denmark from which he compiled comprehensive and highly accurate observations of stars and planets Beginning of the search for a North West Passage
1580	Galileo formulated the laws of the pendulum
1596	Kepler's astronomical calculations supported the theory of Copernicus

The seventeenth century

1600	William Gilbert published his *De Magnete* about magnetism and coined the word 'electricity'
1605	Francis Bacon published *The Advancement of Learning*
1609	Invention of the telescope by a Dutch spectacle-maker
1616	Shakespeare and Cervantes (Don Quixote) died on the same day. Various inventions and discoveries by Galileo: an air thermometer, the compound microscope, Jupiter's moons, sunspots, et al.
1618	Kepler's Laws of Planetary Motion complete
1628	Discovery of the circulation of the blood by William Harvey
1632	Galileo's *Dialogo* published; it favoured Copernicus' theory
1637	Descartes published his philosophy, a search for truth in and through science Atmospheric pressure studied by Torricelli
1651	Hobbes published *The Leviathan*
1660	The Royal Society founded Boyle's discoveries in chemistry
1665	Wave theory of light first suggested to explain Newton's 'rings'
1666	Isaac Newton using 'fluxions,' later found to be identical with Leibniz' calculus
1668	Newton's reflecting telescope

1682	Halley observed the comet which now bears his name
1687	Newton published his *'Principia'*
1690	Locke published *An Essay Concerning Human Understanding*
1697	Stahl first put forward the *phlogiston* theory
1699	Amontons showed that friction between a load and a plane was proportional to the load and independent of the area of surfaces in contact

The eighteenth century

1704	Newton's *Opticks* published, based on a corpuscular theory of light
1710	Berkeley published *Principles of Human Knowledge*
1729	Gray and Wheeler discovered the electric current
1733	The 'flying shuttle' for weaving invented
1747	Franklin put forward a 'single' fluid theory of electricity ('negative' electricity being lack of 'positive') and used the electrical properties of pointed bodies to develop a lightning conductor
1755	Priestley noted that nitrogen oxides are produced by electric sparks in air
1756	Black explained relations between chalk, carbon dioxide, lime, etc. Later, he distinguished between temperature and quantity of heat
1762	Linnaeus classified many plants and animals
1764	Hargreaves invented the 'spinning jenny'
1766	Cavendish identified hydrogen as a distinct gas but thought it originated in metals, not acids
1774	Priestley discovered oxygen Lavoisier formulated his theory of combustion
1776	American 'Declaration of Independence' Adam Smith published *The Wealth of Nations*
1781	A steam engine patented by Watt Kant published *A Critique of Pure Reason*

1789	French Revolution begins
1791	Galvani noticed effect of electricity on frogs' legs Volta began to study such phenomena
1796	First successful vaccination by Jenner
1798	Malthus published *An Essay on Population*
1799	Volta used a 'pile' of cells to produce a large current

The nineteenth century

1800	William Wordsworth lived at Grasmere and produced some of his finest poetry
1807	Lamarck put forward his views on evolution
1808	Dalton published his Atomic Theory
1811	Avogadro coined the word 'molecule'
1815	Davy invented the safety lamp for coal-miners
c. 1817	Young suggested that light moves in transverse waves (beginning of modern wave theory)
1820	Ampere showed that parallel wires carrying electric currents repelled or attracted each other depending on the directions of currents.
1825	Ohm studying electrical resistance
1828	Wohler synthesised urea—hitherto regarded as an 'organic' compound
1831	Faraday studying 'electro-magnetic induction' and
1832	forecast wireless waves, also hinting that light waves might be similar
1839	Becquerel discovered the photo-electric effect (electrical phenomena of some materials induced by light)
1842	Draper first photographed the moon Doppler studying the effect on the frequency (and, therefore, pitch) of sound of the speed of approach or withdrawal of the source of the sound
1847	First use of anaesthetics by Lister
1848	Marx published his *Communist Manifesto*
1849	Fizeau measured the speed of light

1856	Bessemer introduced his methods of steel-making
1859	Darwin published *The Origin of Species*
1863	Huxley published *Evidence of Man's Place in Nature* Kelvin formulated The Laws of Thermodynamics
1865	First use of antiseptics by Lister
1866	Mendel announced his Laws of Heredity First trans-Atlantic cable laid
1869	Mendeleev published his Periodic Table of the chemical elements
1870s	Electric motors and generators being developed Bell invented the telephone
1878	Crookes demonstrated the nature of 'cathode rays'
1885	Pasteur successfully innoculated a boy against rabies
1887	Michelson-Morley experiment failed to detect the 'aether'
1895	Wireless telegraphy successfully established by Marconi Rontgen discovered X-rays Ramsay discovered (on Earth) the gas helium hitherto detected in the sun's spectrum
1898	Becquerel studying radioactivity Pavlov's researches begun
1899	Rutherford studying the nature of α- and β- rays from uranium

The twentieth century

1900	Planck published his 'quantum theory' Binet devised his 'intelligence test' and 'intelligence quotient' (I.Q.)
1905	Einstein published his Special Theory of Relativity
1911–1913	Development of the Rutherford-Bohr model of the atom
1912	Marie Curie isolated the element radium
1913	Freud published his *Interpretation of Dreams*
1915	First transmission of speech by wireless

1919	First transatlantic crossing by air (Alcock and Brown)
1919	Rutherford transmuted nitrogen into oxygen by bombardment with α-particles
1925	First public demonstration of television
1926	Goddard fired the first liquid-fuel rocket
1928	Fleming first observed the effect of a mould on a colony of bacteria — the first step in his discovery of penicillin
1932	Chadwick discovered the sub-atomic particle, the neutron
1938	Nuclear fission first observed; an atom was split, with the release of much energy, when bombarded with neutrons
1942	The first atomic pile built; this emitted a controlled supply of energy from atomic fission
1945	The first atomic bomb used in warfare; this was a 'fission' bomb
1947	Artificial nuclear fusion experiments being carried out; this involved the fusion of two hydrogen nuclei to form a helium nucleus and to emit a large amount of energy
1951	Explosion of the first hydrogen (fusion) bomb
1953	Helicoidal structure of nucleic acids discovered by Watson and Crick
1956	Another sub-atomic particle, the neutrino, discovered at Los Alamos
1957	Artificial nuclear fusion achieved on a tiny scale; the experiments involved very high temperatures and intense magnetic fields. The goal was the controlled release of energy from a cheap and plentiful source — the hydrogen of water.
1959	Karl Popper published *The Logic of Scientific Discovery*
1960	Space probes in use The laser developed
1961	Yuri Gagarin was the first man to travel in space
1962	The first quasar suspected Kuhn published *The Structure of Scientific Revolutions*

1964   Space probe fired from U.S. to Mars

1967   Pulsars discovered
                  First heart transplant

From now on there was a great increase in the exploration of space (Voyager I began surveying Saturn in 1980) and also in the investigation of the atom — with the prospect of yet more new subatomic particles. There was also an increased awareness of the effect of industrial activity on the environment; more and more fossil fuels were being burnt, more forests (which would help to absorb the increased carbon dioxide) were being destroyed, and the supply of unlimited energy from nuclear fusion seemed as far away as ever. In 1989, two chemists announced that they had succeeded in producing nuclear fusion in a test tube — with the emission of neutrons and much energy. For a short, hectic and exciting time, it seemed that the world's energy problems were to be solved. Later, it appeared that, because of the secrecy surrounding their experiments (in case the results were 'stolen' by enterprising businessmen), the chemists had not subjected their work to criticism by physicists who might have been able to reveal that the emission of neutrons was an illusion. (Karl Popper would be able to point out an obvious moral here.)

Meanwhile, the sub-atomic field widens and becomes more bizarre. Some sub-atomic particles have long lifetimes; they exist for more than 10^{-9} seconds. They are called 'strange.' Others—not all detected—seem to have fractional electric charges; they are called 'quarks'—meaning *'nonsense'*—from *Finnegans Wake* by James Joyce. Some of these quarks, unusually, show two types of force and physicists attribute this to something they label 'charm.' Yet more odd behaviour is attributed to qualities labelled 'beauty' and 'truth.' But so far, 'no experimental evidence of their existence has been revealed!'

Things to Do

The grouping of these suggestions does not always correspond to chapters in the book, and teachers who use them will obviously select those which best match the current curiosity of the class. In any case, the list is not exhaustive and teachers will want to add their own investigations. The important thing is that the activities should be *investigations*; I have written the suggestions in this form, left many of them open-ended (solutions to be found in text-books!), and would recommend that teachers subtly lead their students to come to their own conclusions. If they are 'wrong,' further examination will soon reveal their wrongness; if they are 'right,' perhaps it's because we haven't done enough investigations.

Discovery of metals

Heat copper carbonate. What happens? Can we identify the gas emitted? Try dissolving the cold residue in dilute sulphuric acid. The solution may yield crystals (see later).

Heat some of the black residue with powdered carbon. After prolonged heating (and cooling), the new residue does not dissolve in dilute sulphuric acid; what sort of change has taken place? Try dissolving it in moderately concentrated nitric acid; compare the reaction with the dissolving of copper in the same acid.

Put an iron or steel nail into copper sulphate solution. What happens? Put some copper into iron sulphate solution. What does not happen? What can you say about the 'activity' of copper compared with that of iron? What has this got to do with the Bronze Age and the Iron Age? Discuss how metals may have been first isolated.

Other early discoveries

Drag a cylinder (a pencil will do) over the surface of a table. Then roll it. Use several pencils to transport a heavy book from one point to another. Discuss how the wheel may have been invented.

Investigate friction. Try to establish simple laws. Discuss advantages and disadvantages.

Investigate other simple machines such as levers and pulley systems. Why were they so important to primitive humans? How could they gradually increase human intelligence?

The need to measure

Holding a metre rule at one end, try to touch a small, distant object with the other end '(a) when closing one eye, (b) with both eyes open. What can you say about the use of both eyes in estimating distance?

Prepare various packages in which varying amounts of sand are contained in small volumes (e.g., matchboxes) and in large (e.g., plastic bags). Try to arrange them in order of weight without using a balance.

Without using a measuring cylinder, try to estimate volumes of liquid in containers of varied size and shape.

Put some hot, ice-cold, and tepid water into three separate beakers. Immerse the index finger of each hand in the beakers with hot and cold water for half-a-minute. Then transfer both fingers to the tepid water. What do you notice?

Without using a thermometer, try to compare the temperatures of various rooms in different circumstances (e.g., having just been running hard, sitting still, in warm conditions, in cold conditions).

Without using a watch, try to estimate time spans, large and small, in different circumstances (e.g., when looking forward to the end of a class, when fully interested in one's work!).

Measure the circumferences and diameters of, say, ten circular objects. Calculate the ratio Circumference/Diameter. Find the average value of the hundreds of results from a class. How close is the result to the accepted value of π?

Some experiments connected with Galileo

Drop a series of heavy and light objects from the same height. Can you make any generalization about the times of fall? Compare the times of fall of a coin and a small scrap of paper (a) when they are falling separately, (b) when the paper is resting on the coin. Is there anything holding back both objects, but the paper more than the coin? Can you devise other experiments to test your theory?

Investigate the pendulum. How does the time of swing depend on (a) the weight of the bob (the heavy mass suspended by thread)? (b) the angle through which the pendulum swings? (c) the length of the pendulum (from point of suspension to centre of gravity of the bob)?

Make a simple water clock (in which a steady stream of water pours from a large container). Under what conditions can you estimate time from (a) the rate of emission of drops?, (b) the amount of water emitted? How could you make these times as reliable as possible?

Time marbles rolling down inclined planes onto a horizontal table. Can you find a relationship between the distance travelled down the plane and the time taken? With the same inclined plane and the same distance of fall, measure how far the marble goes over the table when the table surface is covered with paper of varying roughness. The marble goes farthest when the table is smooth; what would happen if there were no friction or air resistance?

It can be shown that, in free fall after 1, 2, 3, 4 seconds, a stone will drop 4.9m, 19.6m, 44.1m, 78.4m. Assuming that a projectile fired horizontally from a cliff-top falls at the same rate as the stone while travelling horizontally with an undiminished speed of 20m per second, draw a graph to show the path of the projectile. Repeat the exercise for different horizontal speeds (say, 40ms^{-1}, 60ms^{-1}) and compare your results with Newton's 'thought experiment.'

Things don't always behave as you expect

You expect the circular tin to roll down the inclined plane (Figure A). But if a lump of lead is taped inside, and if it is placed on the plane as shown, it will roll up.

FIGURE A

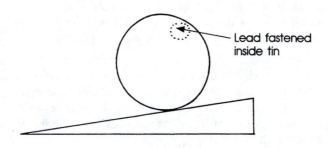

Lead fastened inside tin

FIGURE B

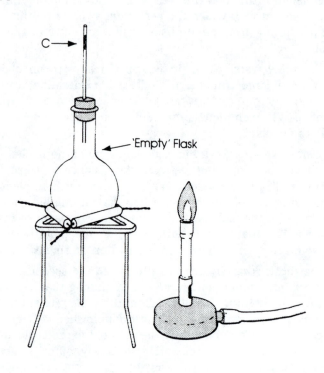

C→

'Empty' Flask

Does air expand on heating? If so, you expect the small column of water (C) to move away from the flask when the flask is heated (Figure B). And it does. But something else happens first. Why?

You can establish simple rules for floating and sinking: if an object weighs more than an equal volume of water, it will sink in water; if it weighs less, it will float. So, since water expands when it is heated, it should 'float' (or rise) in cold water, and, conversely, cooling water will 'sink' in surrounding warmer water. You can devise experiments to test these statements.

But what about ice? Logic would predict that ice should sink in water, but it clearly does not. Since it floats, it must expand before it freezes. Can we demonstrate this? Discuss the consequences of this expansion; they range from burst water pipes to the climate of the whole planet (think of the results of icebergs sinking to the bottom of the oceans).

And what about thin sheets of metal which float on the surface of water? But what happens when we push them below the surface?

Is there some sort of force at the surface which holds them up? Add some detergent to the water and see what happens to the floating sheets. Can this force have anything to do with the formation of 'packages' of water which we call 'drops'? Or with 'capillary rise' — the term describing the rise of water in tubes of narrow bore? Since this rise will depend on the size of the force, can you devise experiments which would show the effect of adding increasing amounts of detergent to water?

More about carbon dioxide and carbonates

We can compare samples of water for 'hardness' by shaking them with soap powder and comparing the amounts of lather produced. We probably know that, when hard water is boiled, it turns cloudy because 'chalk' (calcium carbonate) is precipitated. But how does the chalk get into the water in the first place when it is insoluble?

Pass carbon dioxide into a solution of calcium hydroxide in water. What happens first? But what happens later? If the first cloudiness was the formation of calcium carbonate, could calcium carbonate still be present at the end of the passage of carbon dioxide? And if the heating of hard water simply reverses this experiment, we ought to see something else apart from the precipitation of chalk. Investigate other means of producing carbon dioxide, including brewing (with yeast) and baking (with yeast or sodium hydrogen carbonate). Discuss its role in these processes. Explore, too, these reactions in the context of acids, bases, and salts.

At present, the most notorious means of production of carbon dioxide is the burning of fossil fuels. How can we show that the gas *is* produced when, say, natural gas is burned? When we ignite natural gas we also notice a 'dampness.' Is this water? How could we be certain? And where does it come from? If it comes from the natural gas itself we could show its presence *before* the burning. Is this possible? Could the dampness come from the air? If so, why does it appear only when the natural gas is burned? Could the dampness be formed when the gas is burned? If so, how? What does this reveal about the elements present in natural gas? Why is the gas an example of a hydrocarbon? How could we show that there are no other elements present?

Prediction from Mendeleev's Periodic Table

Can you see, from this section of the Periodic Table (Figure C), that it is possible to predict that bromine is likely to be a liquid, orange-red in colour, with an atomic weight around 80, melting point

FIGURE C

Group VII of Mendeleev's Periodic Table					
	State at normal temperatures	Colour	Atomic weight	Melting point (°C)	Boiling point (°C)
Fluorine	gas	pale-yellow	19	-223	-182
Chlorine	gas	greenish-yellow	35.5	-104	-34
Bromine	?	?	?	?	?
Iodine	solid	black	127	114	184

about 0°C, and boiling point about 70°C? Compare these predictions with the actual properties of bromine.

The Atomic Theory

Think of a balance with a shallow pan; the pan is hidden from the eye but we can see the scale. Objects are thrown at the pan; some stay there, others fall off, a few are pushed off at each throw. Readings on the scale after a series of 'throws' are: 36.4g, 54.6g, 9.1g, 63.7g, 27.3g, 81.9g. Can you see that it is possible to infer that (a) the objects are all equal in size? (b) each *probably* weighs 9.1g but could possibly weigh 4.55g? What has this to do with the Atomic Theory?

Some experiments on light

Using the laws of reflection we can predict mathematically that the image in a plane mirror is as far behind the mirror as the object is in front (Figure D). If we try to confirm this experimentally, using a mirror with a protective sheet of glass over its reflecting surface, we may find an error. Is this due to faulty measurement? Or something else which we haven't taken into account?

Investigate *refraction* first with a block of glass with parallel faces. Then predict the passage of a ray of light through a 60° glass prism. Test your predictions experimentally. What else do you see?

FIGURE D

a)

b)

Where does the colour come from? Examine the spectrum of white light with colour filters. Do these filters *add* colour? Or subtract?

With compasses, draw an arc of a circle to represent a concave reflecting surface (Figure E). Geometrically, find the focus of parallel rays of light. Confirm with concave spherical mirrors. Discuss application to astronomical telescope devised by Newton, and to tv dish aerials.

Investigate lenses; make simple refracting telescopes. Why did Newton need to devise a *reflecting* telescope?

Some experiments in sound

Investigate origins and transmission. In particular, examine the sounds produced by a stretched string when its length is halved, quartered, divided in ratio 1:2, etc. Look up Pythagoras' experiments and connections.

FIGURE E

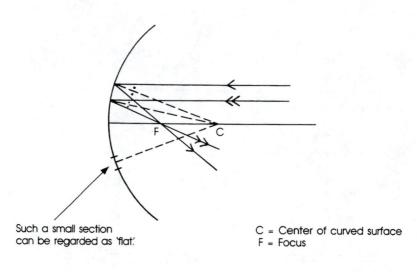

Such a small section
can be regarded as 'flat.'

C = Center of curved surface
F = Focus

Investigate echoes as sound 'images.' Show, with microphone and tape recorder, that sound can be focussed like light from a concave surface (some dustbin lids may provide the correct curvature).

Estimate the speed of sound using echoes. Find a wall which will produce a sharp echo of a hand-clap. Clap again so that the second clap obscures the echo of the first. Repeat the clapping so that you never hear the echoes. Time twenty or more claps and calculate the interval of time between successive claps. Knowing the distance which sound has travelled in this interval (twice the distance from where you stand to the wall) calculate the speed of sound.

Some experiments in electricity and magnetism

Rub different plastics and investigate attraction (of small pieces of paper) and repulsion (between same plastics, similarly rubbed). In particular, observe the effect of rubbed plastic on a thin stream of water from a tap.

Use simple low-voltage circuits (including a lamp) to investigate conductors and insulators. In particular, is water a conductor? What sort of solutions conduct? What happens when they do
conduct?

Investigate magnets. Examine the magnetic effect of an electric current. If possible, 'invent' a simple electric motor.

Show links here with crystal formation (earlier). Show the difference between throwing a handful of nails on a bench and throwing a handful of magnets.

Discuss entropy — if possible, by clips from films which (running backwards) show exploded, demolished buildings resuming their former shape. This is not expected; neither is the constant geometrical shape of copper sulphate crystals emerging from solution. We must have overlooked something. By comparison with the nail/magnet demonstration and by other information gleaned from the above experiments, suggest an explanation.

Some other points for discussion

Collect and discuss superstitions; to what extent can their persistence be explained by coincidence? If B follows A, this does not mean that A caused B. Discuss with regard to the moon's phases and (a) the menstrual cycle, (b) the tides.

Discuss the 'proof' that $6 = 7$ (Figure F). We may say that we are not 'allowed' to 'divide across' by $(x-5)$ i.e., zero. But why not?

We can show that the three angles of a triangle add up to 180° by tearing off the three corners of a paper triangle and fitting them together. But consider this problem: an explorer set off from a camp P and travelled 100 miles south to A; then he travelled 100 miles east to B; finally he travelled 100 miles north. If he then arrived back at P, where is P? It is impossible to represent this on a flat surface — just as impossible as drawing a triangle containing two right angles — but in practice, on the Earth's surface where P is the North Pole, it works (Figure G).

FIGURE F

$$\text{Suppose } 5 = x$$
$$\text{Then } x - 5 = 0$$
$$x + 1 = 6$$
$$x + 2 = 7$$
$$(x-5)(x+1) = 0$$
$$(x-5)(x+2) = 0$$
$$\text{So, } (x-5)(x+1) = (x-5)(x+2)$$

Since $(x-5)$ appears on both sides of the equation, the other factors must also be equal;

$$\text{i.e. } (x+1) = (x+2)$$
$$\text{or } 6 = 7$$

FIGURE G

a)

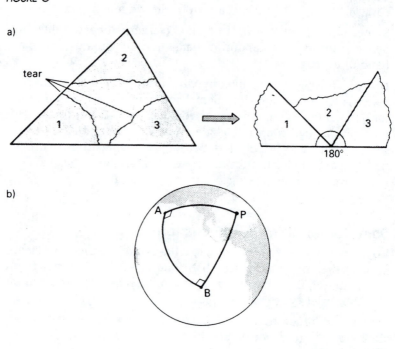

b)

FIGURE H

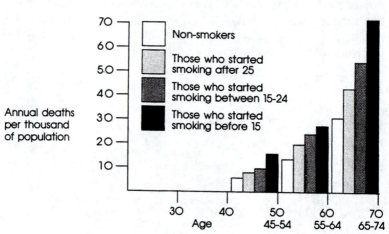

Figure H shows the number of deaths per year per 1000 American men at various ages according to the age of starting to smoke. In other words, it shows 'facts' with no suggestion of cause or effect and no explanation. But we can use these facts to start speculating, theorizing and, most important of all, to initiate further investigation. Can you come to any important conclusions from such facts?

Suggestions for Further Reading

General

Bronowski, Jacob. 1978. *Common Sense of Science*. Cambridge, Mass.: Harvard University Press.

_____. 1972. *Science and Human Values*. New York: Harper & Row.

_____. 1974. *The Ascent of Man*. Boston, Mass.: Little, Brown & Co.

_____. and Bruce Mazlish. n.d. *Western Intellectual Tradition: From Leonardo to Hegel*. New York: Harper & Row.

Darwin, Charles. 1982. *The Origin of Species*. Edited by J. W. Burrow. New York: Penguin.

Davies, Paul. 1980. *Other Worlds*. New York: Penguin

Dawkins, Richard. 1988. *The Blind Watchmaker*. New York: Norton.

Feynman, Richard P. 1986. *Surely You're Joking, Mr. Feynman*. New York: Bantam.

Koestler, Arthur. 1959. *The Sleepwalkers*. New York: Penguin.

McKenzie, A. E. *1988. Major Achievements of Science: The Development of Science From Ancient Times to the Present*. Ames, Iowa: Iowa State University Press.

Medawar, Peter. 1988. Limits of Science. Oxford Univ. Press.

Miller, Jonathan. 1981. *The Body in Question*. New York: Random.

Postman, Neil, and Charles Weingartner. 1987. *Teaching as a Subversive Activity*. New York: Dell.

Facts

Chesterton, G. K. 1987. *The Complete Father Brown*. New York: Penguin.

Doyle, Arthur Conan. 1986. *Sherlock Holmes: The Complete Novels & Stories, Vols. 1 and 2*. New York: Bantam.

Huff, Darrell, and Irving Geis. 1954. *How to Lie with Statistics*. New York: Norton.

————. 1964. *How to Take a Chance*. New York: Norton.

Kennedy, Ludovic. 1985. *10, Rillington Place*. New York: Avon.

Weinberg. 1988. *The First Three Minutes: A Modern View of the Origin of the Universe*. New York: Basic.

Fancies

Bulfinch, Thomas. 1959. *Bulfinch's Mythology*. New York: Dell.

Campbell, Joseph, and Bill Moyers. 1988. *The Power of Myth*. New York: Doubleday.

Crombie, A. C. 1979. *Augustine to Galileo*. Cambridge, Mass.: Harvard University Press.

De Bono, Edward. *Lateral Thinking*. n.d. New Rochelle, N.Y.: International Center for Creative Thinking.

Farrington, Benjamin. 1981. *Greek Science*. Chester Springs, Pa.: Dufour.

Frazer, James G. 1985. *The Golden Bough*. rev,. abr. ed. New York: Macmillan.

Jung, Carl G. 1968. *Man and His Symbols*. New York: Dell.

————. 1965. *Memories, Dreams, Reflections*. Edited by Aniela Jaffe. New York: Random House.

————.1984. *Psychology and Western Religion*. Princeton, N.J.: Princeton University Press.

Kitto, H. D. 1988. *The Greeks*. Magnolia, Mass.: Peter Smith.

Pirsig, Robert M. 1976. *Zen and the Art of Motorcycle Maintenance*. New York: Bantam.

Toulmin, Stephen and June Goodfield. *The Fabric of the Heavens: The Development of Astronomy and Dynamics*. New York: Harper & Row.

Trevor-Roper, Hugh R. 1969. *European Witch Craze in the 16th and 17th Centuries & Other Essays*. New York: Harper & Row.

Experiments

Brecht, Bertold. 1966. *Galileo*. Edited by Eric Bentley. Translated by Charles Laughton. New York: Grove.

Magee, Bryan. 1973. *Popper*. Fontana.

Santillana, Giorgio. 1955. *Crime of Galileo*. Chicago: University of Chicago Press.

Predictions

Copleston, F. C. 1956. *Aquinas*. New York: Penguin.

Dawkins, Richard. 1976. *The Selfish Gene*. New York: Oxford

University Press.

Koestler, Arthur. 1973. *The Case of the Midwife Toad*. New York: Random House.

Stafford-Clark, David. 1971. *What Freud Really Said*. New York: Schocken.

Toulmin, Stephen, and June Goodfield. 1983. *The Discovery of Time*. New York: Hippocrene Books.

Watson, James D. 1969. *The Double Helix*. New York: New American Library

Models

Cervantes, Miguel Saavedra De. 1951. *Don Quixote*. Translated by John M. Cohen. New York: Penguin.

Gould, Stephen J. 1983. *The Mismeasure of Man*. New York: Norton.

Kuhn, Thomas S. 1970. *The Structure of Scientific Revolutions*, 2d ed. Chicago: University of Chicago Press.

Monod, Jacques. 1972. *Chance and Necessity*. New York: Random.

Thurber, James. 1983. *The Secret Life of Walter Mitty*. Mankato, Minn.: Creative Education Inc.

Effects

Asimov, Isaac. 1978. *The Tragedy of the Moon*. New York: Dell.

Boorstin, Daniel J. 1984. *The Image: A Guide to Pseudo-Events in America*. Magnolia, Mass.: Peter Smith.

Childe, Gordon V. 1983. *Man Makes Himself*. New York: New American Library.

Huxley, Aldous. 1970. *The Perennial Philosophy*. New York: Harper & Row.

Lewis, Clive S. 1968. *The Discarded Image*. New York: Cambridge University Press.

Popper, Karl R. 1966. *The Open Society and Its Enemies*. Princeton, N.J.: Princeton University Press.

Warnock, G. J. 1983. *Berkeley*. Notre Dame, Ind.: University of Notre Dame Press.

Doubts

Calder, Nigel. 1980. *Einstein's Universe*. New York: Penguin.

Capra, Fritjof. 1984. *The Tao of Physics*. New York: Bantam.

Close, Frank. 1983. *The Cosmic Onion: Quarks and the Nature of the Universe*. New York: American Institute of Physics.

Dyson, Freeman. 1988. *Disturbing the Universe*. New York: Ticknor & Fields.

Heisenberg, Werner. n.d. *Physics and Beyond*. New York: Harper & Row.

Jungk, Robert. 1970. *Brighter than 1000 Suns: A Personal History of the Atomic Scientists*. San Diego, Calif.: Harcourt Brace Jovanovich.

Koestler, Arthur. 1973. *The Roots of Coincidence*. New York: Random House.

Laing, Ronald D. 1965. *The Divided Self*. New York: Penguin.

Schell, Jonathan. 1982. *The Fate of the Earth*. New York: Avon.

Zukav, Gary. 1984. *The Dancing Wu Li Masters: An Overview of the New Physics*. New York: Bantam

Integration

Berman, Morris. 1981. *The Reenchantment of the World*. Ithaca, N.Y.: Cornell University Press.

James, William. 1984. *Varieties of Religious Experience: A Study in Human Nature*. Edited by Martin E. Marty. New York: Pilgrim.

Koestler, Arthur. 1964. *The Act of Creation*. New York: Penguin.

Popper, Karl. 1985. *Unended Quest: An Intellectual Autobiography*. rev. ed. Peru, Illinois.: Open Court.

Russell, Bertrand. 1971. *Conquest of Happiness*. New York: Liveright.

Stevens, Anthony. 1990. *On Jung*. New York: Routledge.

Storr, Anthony. 1989. *Churchill's Black Dog, Kafka's Mice and other Phenomena of the Human Mind*. New York: Grove.

Van der Post, Laurens. 1977. *Jung and The Story of Our Time*. New York: Random House.

Index